GEORGE ORWELL
SELECTED WRITINGS

GEORGE ORWELL

Selected Writings

EDITED BY
GEORGE BOTT

HEINEMANN EDUCATIONAL BOOKS

LONDON

Heinemann Educational Books Ltd

LONDON EDINBURGH MELBOURNE AUCKLAND TORONTO
SINGAPORE HONG KONG KUALA LUMPUR
NAIROBI IBADAN JOHANNESBURG
NEW DELHI

ISBN O 435 13675 5
INTRODUCTION AND NOTES © GEORGE BOTT 1958
FIRST PUBLISHED 1958
REPRINTED 1960, 1962, 1963, 1964, 1965, 1966, 1968,
1969 (twice), 1970, 1972

PUBLISHED BY
HEINEMANN EDUCATIONAL BOOKS LTD
48 CHARLES STREET, LONDON WIX 8AH
PRINTED IN GREAT BRITAIN BY MORRISON AND GIBB LTD
LONDON AND EDINBURGH

CONTENTS

PREFACE

THIS selection of George Orwell's writings is intended mainly for sixth forms, adult classes and training college students; I hope, too, that it will be studied by those post G.C.E. "O" level pupils who stay at school for one year. They are notoriously difficult to cater for and Orwell offers a base for the exploration of so many fields: politics, social problems, foreign affairs, prose style, for example.

In this variety lies one of the reasons for compiling this book. Orwell discusses many of the aspects of life that boys and girls think seriously about from the age of, say, fifteen; and his honesty and sincerity—words that crop up again and again when Orwell is being discussed—make him exceptional among political writers.

I have tried to show something of Orwell as a political apologist; something of his remarkable ability to record experience vividly and to argue convincingly; some autobiography, some literary criticism, some satire. These examples of his writing are only tasters: his independent, restless, probing mind can best be seen at work in his full-length books. If, as a result of this selection, young readers discover Orwell, I shall be more than satisfied.

My thanks are due to Mrs. Orwell and to Messrs. Martin Secker and Warburg Ltd. for permission to use copyright material; to Mr. Robert Conquest and the Editor of *The Listener* for permission to print the poem "George Orwell"; to the Librarians and Staffs of Cumberland County Library and Keswick District Library for their customary unfailing assistance and courtesy; to various friends and libraries for suggestions and the loan of books; to Mr. A. R. Beal for his gentle but firm encouragement; and to my wife for help in countless ways.

G. B.

GEORGE ORWELL

Moral and mental glaciers melting slightly
Betray the influence of his warm intent.
Because he taught us what the actual meant
The vicious winter grips its prey less tightly.

Not all were grateful for his help, one finds,
For how they hated him, who huddled with
The comfort of a quick remedial myth
Against the cold world and their colder minds.

We die of words. For touchstones he restored
The real person, real event or thing;
—And thus we see not war but suffering
As the conjunction to be most abhorred.

He shared with a great world, for greater ends,
That honesty, a curious cunning virtue
You share with just the few who won't desert you,
A dozen writers, half-a-dozen friends.

A moral genius. And truth-seeking brings
Sometimes a silliness we view askance,
Like Darwin playing his bassoon to plants;
He too had lapses, but he claimed no wing.

While those who drown a truth's empiric part
In dithyramb or dogma turn frenetic;
—Than whom no writer could be less poetic
He left this lesson for all verse, all art.

                                    ROBERT CONQUEST

INTRODUCTION

"My subject, George Orwell, is of the English war and post-war writers, not alone the one most worthy of attention, but he is the only one."—Wyndham Lewis. *The Writer and the Absolute*. Methuen, 1952.

GEORGE ORWELL was born at Motihari in 1903. His father, an official in the Opium Department of the Indian Customs and Excise, retired on a small pension when Orwell was very young and the family left Bengal for England.

The pension was barely adequate to keep up appearances and Orwell soon discovered that in such shabby-genteel families as his own there was "far more *consciousness* of poverty than in any working-class family above the level of the dole". He became acutely aware of social differences, later confessing that his family belonged to the "lower-upper-middle-class . . . the layer of society lying between £2000 and £300 a year: my own family was not far from the bottom".

As a child, a lonely child affected by bad health, Orwell found difficulties in personal relationships which aggravated the night-mare of rent, clothes and school bills that haunted his parents. His father and mother were remote figures as he grew up: "Looking back on childhood after the infant years were over, I do not believe that I ever felt love for any mature person, except my mother, and even her I did not trust, in the sense that shyness made me conceal most of my real feeling from her. . . . I merely disliked my own father, whom I had barely seen before I was eight and who appeared to me simply as a gruff-voiced elderly man forever saying 'Don't'."

NOTE. This introduction is not intended to be a full critical survey of Orwell. Using Orwell's autobiographical material freely, I want to give the main facts about his life, link them with his books and by the comments of others as well as my own provide the reader with a few lines of thought to follow. Three full-length studies of Orwell have been published; details of these and of Orwell's works are given in the bibliography. I should like to acknowledge with gratitude my considerable debt to all of them.

3

In 1911, the year he first read *Gulliver's Travels*, Orwell went to an exclusive preparatory school on the south coast. He was allowed to attend at reduced fees as one of a special group of bright boys who were crammed and if necessary flogged for scholarships to Eton, Harrow and other public schools.

Most of the pupils were the sons of rich parents and Orwell, like Gordon Comstock in *Keep the Aspidistra Flying*, soon realized that he was an outsider. Apart from receiving less pocket-money than the other boys and constantly being reminded of his penury, he was hounded by the headmaster's wife, before whom "one seemed as helpless as a snake before a snake-charmer". She once said to Orwell in front of the whole school: "You know you're not going to grow up with money, don't you? Your people aren't rich. You must learn to be sensible. Don't get above yourself!" The humiliation of it: no wonder Orwell saw life as a series of money rackets. Such, such were the joys of schooldays; *Such, Such were the Joys* is the title of Orwell's essay on his schooldays, unfortunately not published in this country.

Orwell won scholarships to both Eton and Wellington but he left Crossgates, as he called the school (it is the St. Wulfric's of Cyril Connolly's *Enemies of Promise*) scarred for life by his sufferings. "I had no money, I was weak, I was ugly, I was unpopular, I had a chronic cough, I was cowardly, I smelt. . . . The conviction that it was *not possible* for me to be a success went deep enough to influence my actions till far on into adult life. Until I was thirty I always planned my life on the assumption not only that any major undertaking was bound to fail, but that I could only expect to live a few years longer."

The importance of money wedged itself firmly in young Orwell's mind. At an early age, he determined that he would make £100,000 which would yield an income of £4000 and buy all the cars, houses and estates that his school-friends boasted of. The alternative was "to become a little office boy at £40 a year" and that he resolved to avoid. In fact, neither alternative materialized. With rather more acumen, Orwell knew from the age of five or six that he wanted to be a writer and, fortune or on fortune, that was what he did become.

Orwell chose Eton. The demon of the empty purse was still gnawing at him but there was no longer the slavery of cramming for a scholarship; so he relaxed. Of the years he spent at Eton he wrote: "I did not work there and learned very little and I don't feel that Eton has been much of a formative influence in my life." But he admitted in an article in the *Observer* in 1948 that Eton had "a tolerant and civilized atmosphere which gives each boy a fair chance of developing his own individuality".

This was just the atmosphere Orwell wanted and although Eton perhaps did not influence him greatly academically, the contact with the minds and personalities of his contemporaries— Cyril Connolly, Richard Rees and John Strachey, for example— was invaluable for him.

At the age of fifteen he was immersed in *The Way of all Flesh* and the atheistic arguments of *Androcles and the Lion*; he was a rebel among a rebellious generation of schoolboys, inspired and nurtured by his wide reading of H. G. Wells, John Galsworthy and Bernard Shaw. The influence of Wells was particularly strong and remained to shape even his last two books.

The character of Eton in Orwell's day is illustrated in the following story. A general knowledge paper given to the boys contained the question: "Whom do you consider the ten greatest men now living?" Fifteen of the sixteen boys answering the paper included Lenin among their ten. It would be interesting to see the choice of present-day Etonians.

When the time came for him to leave Eton, Orwell did not take the normal step of going to a university, although he could probably have won a scholarship had he wished. Mr. Tom Hopkinson says that Orwell was advised by one of his tutors to find a job abroad, make plenty of money, and at the age of forty retire and choose whatever way of life appealed to him.

Acting on this advice, Orwell joined the Indian Imperial Police and served in Burma from 1922 to 1927. His experiences are embodied in *Burmese Days*, a hard-hitting, over-contemptuous condemnation of British imperial administration and administrators written under the ache of disillusionment and frustration.

Outwardly Orwell acted the Sahib, shouldering the White Man's Burden efficiently; inwardly he was obviously embarrassed and unhappy, disapproving of his job, smarting at the social pharisaism, depressed by the absence of freedom, particularly freedom to say what he really thought. Malcolm Muggeridge considers, however, that it is an oversimplification to say that Orwell was revolted by his police duties; he feels that "there was a Kiplingesque side to his character which made him romanticize the Raj and its mystique" and that the picture of the European community in *Burmese Days* is exaggerated and unreal.

But there is no doubt that the lash of authority he wielded stung Orwell himself. "I never went into jail," he wrote, "without feeling that my place was really on the other side of the bars." Certainly no young man with a conscience like Orwell's could happily accept the tyranny of an imperialist police force over a native population; "not only were we hanging people and putting them into jail and so forth; we were doing it in the capacity of unwanted foreign invaders".

In 1927 Orwell came back to England: "I was already half determined to throw up the job, and one sniff of English air decided me." Not that he stayed to breathe the air he loved—Orwell was intensely patriotic: "the deepest of all Orwell's emotions," writes Christopher Hollis, "was his overwhelming love of England"—instead he went to Paris and lost himself among the very dregs of society.

For a time he toyed with writing, living presumably on his leave pay and savings; when his money gave out, he worked as a dish-washer, living and drudging in the most sordid and filthy conditions. From Paris he returned to England, to a comparable existence in doss-houses and "spikes". Friends would willingly have helped him, as they did in the end, but Orwell was resolute.

Various reasons have been suggested for this plunge from the respectable heights of Eton and the British community in Burma into the gutters of humanity. As an act of deliberate, calculated mortification, it is one of the keys to Orwell's character, and what he and his friends have had to say about it is helpful in understanding the man and the development of his ideas.

There was, first of all, a sense of deep guilt over Burma. One need not go so far as Mr. Hollis and imagine Orwell was haunted by an acute sense of sin; but Burma had left him restless and brooding. "For five years," he writes, "I had been part of an oppressive system and it left me with a bad conscience. . . . I was conscious of an immense weight of guilt that I had got to expiate." Not only the underworld of Paris and the doss-houses of London but the writing of *Burmese Days* also helped in the expiation; the landscapes of Burma were a torment that *had* to be written about.

Perhaps Orwell wanted to test himself. His friend, Sir Richard Rees, has noted that Orwell "had only to think of something that would be beyond endurance and he could not rest until he had set himself the task of enduring it". This, too, would fit the facts: Orwell intentionally went to the dogs—he himself uses the cliché in this connexion—and forced himself to put up with dirt, smells, poverty and hunger.

He may have chosen the way of poverty to find a peace of mind in the comfort of an uncomplicated life; he soon found that being a pauper meant "complicated meanness" and pretence, with one redeeming feature: it annihilates the future. Possibly this choice was one of several evils facing him; 1927 was a year of slump and unemployment and Orwell had very little money, few connexions, fewer qualifications and the chances of finding a suitable job were remote.

Above all, Orwell was possessed by an anxiety to identify himself with the oppressed, "to take upon himself a share of the burden of the sins of the world," as Mr. Brander puts it. "These (that is, tramps, criminals, beggars, prostitutes) were 'the lowest of the low', and these were the people," wrote Orwell, "with whom I wanted to get into contact. What I profoundly wanted, at that time, was to find some way of getting out of the respectable world altogether." Having in Burma been identified with the oppressors, he now wanted to be identified with the oppressed; any kind of success, he thought, was a form of bullying, failure was the only virtue.

One wonders, too, whether a tiny voice whispered to Orwell that in this strange other-world he would discover plenty of material for a book. A book did in fact come out of it; *Down and Out in Paris and London* was published in 1933. In spite of high praise it sold badly, as did all Orwell's books until *Animal Farm*. The first part, written in prose as gay and lively as Paris itself, is warm with teeming life and extraordinary characters; the London part is greyer, more serious: the tramps and unemployed are drab, the charity of the Salvation Army and the churches, like their tea, is weak and cheerless, the casual wards are dismal and depressing.

From 1929 Orwell kept himself not so much by writing, though he did contribute to various periodicals, as by a series of jobs which provided a little money and plenty of material to be woven into his later books. He worked as a tutor and as a teacher in private schools; he was a bookshop assistant; he kept a chicken farm, a village store and a public house.

About this time he adopted the pen-name by which he is universally known, Orwell being a river in Suffolk near which he once lived. His real name was Eric Arthur Blair and it is said that he disliked it because it betrayed his Scottish origin. Scotland had been anathema to him since his Crossgates days when his rich friends made him feel horribly inferior by their talk of deer-forests and Scottish holidays. He told T. R. Fyvel that he did not like "Eric" because of its Norse associations with the sentimental stories of his childhood. These are strange irrationalities in one so normally sane and sensible; but the change of name may well symbolize two things—a deliberate rejection of the unhappy memories of Eric Blair's miserable boyhood; and Orwell's intense love for England. What could be more English than a Suffolk river and the Christian name of England's Patron Saint?

His next two novels, *A Clergyman's Daughter* (1935) and *Keep the Aspidistra Flying* (1936), are both semi-autobiographical. They are by no means great novels, though they are fired, in Sir Compton Mackenzie's words, by "directness, vigour, courage and vitality".

Naturally Orwell's novels cannot be ignored, but his best writing, and his most significant, is in other media—reporting, autobiography, satire, essays. The characters of his novels are flat (in the E. M. Forster sense) and are usually little more than convenient Aunt Sallies battered by some social injustice or other; his plots lack tension and proceed by hops, skips and jumps instead of jog-trots and sprints; his selection of material is frequently not dictated by the demands of his story but by a strong desire to rub the reader's nose in some pet theory.

A Clergyman's Daughter and *Keep the Aspidistra Flying* are imaginative tracts, the one on religion, the other on money; Orwell, very much a Monday-schoolteacher, disguising a serious lesson inside a loosely-contrived satirical story. The description of Mrs. Creevy's school, the hop picking, Dorothy Hare's night in Trafalgar Square, Gordon and Rosemary at Crickham-on-Thames are much more striking and memorable than any conflict or development of character.

In 1936 Orwell became a professed Socialist. This did not mean that he did his tricks at the crack of a party whip; freedom of thought and action was as essential to him as the air he breathed: without it, writing was impossible, his passionate devotion to truth a mockery. He never wavered in his faith that genuine Socialism—his own brand, that is—was the only hope for a better world. Perhaps bouncing round his mind was an echo of Stephen Spender's remark that "a writer to-day who wishes to produce the best work he is capable of producing, must first of all become a socialist, must go over to the progressive side of this class conflict".

Orwell's first steps along the road to Socialism took him to Wigan. Invited by the publisher, Victor Gollancz, to write a report on one of the depressed area of England, he went north to the squalor of Lancashire.

His book, *The Road to Wigan Pier* (1937), in spite of many faults, gives a vivid and disturbing picture of working-class life in a town where more than one person in three was out of work. Accepting stoically the bug bites and black beetles, Orwell lived in a dingy lodging-house, poked his nose into everything, and sent to Mr. Gollancz a manuscript that caused a considerable flutter in the Left Wing strongholds.

The book was the March 1937 choice of the Left Book Club but Gollancz found it necessary to write a strong criticism of it on behalf of himself and his fellow selectors, John Strachey and Harold Laski. He admitted that it was a long time since he had read so living a book, or one so full of a burning indignation against poverty and oppression, but warned his readers of the highly provocative remarks Orwell made. Gollancz had marked well over a hundred passages about which he wanted to argue. He objected, for example, to Orwell's statement that most Socialists were stupid, offensive and insincere; or to his slighting references to vegetarians and pacifists.

The weeks he spent in Wigan were Orwell's first real contact with the working classes; they remained his major interest and he spared nothing in his fight to improve their conditions of life and labour. But there is some truth in the criticism that he tended to sentimentalize them, to see them, as Richard Hoggart puts it in *The Uses of Literacy*, "through the cosy fug of an Edwardian music-hall". He almost cowers with shame at a family background and a school which had taught him to despise the black-handed workers and saves himself by a bitter tirade in the second part of *The Road to Wigan Pier* against class distinctions. He calls for Socialism to be humanized, to be built on the triple foundations of liberty, justice and common decency.

These three abstractions are constantly cropping up in Orwell's writings; they are tags which any orator can toss about to gain applause, it is true, but they are nevertheless fundamental to an understanding of Orwell. Socialism for him was not closely argued dialectics or academic debate, but a positive if rather vague drive towards brotherly love and honourable equality. Decency, after all, must include such qualities as honesty, fair dealing, sympathy, kindness, concern for others; and are not these as important as material progress, economic theories and full production?

However wrong or misguided Orwell might have been, *The Road to Wigan Pier* is not a book to ignore. The second part contains an important autobiographical account of the author's schooldays; and the book as a whole is the angry outcry of a man who did not merely talk about social abuses but dived headlong into them, even though, as John Beavan has suggested, Orwell attacked the class barrier at its thickest and highest point.

This inability to be a passive bystander which had driven him to Paris and Wigan, now drove him and his wife, Eileen O'Shaughnessy, whom he had married in 1937, to Spain.

In Spain the civil war was raging. Franco, helped by the Axis Fascists, was fighting against the Spanish Republic, which was ardently supported by the Spanish workers who saw the war as the spear-head of a revolution. Orwell went to write newspaper articles about the war but instead joined the militia to fight, as he put it, against Fascism and for common decency. He avoided the Communist International Brigade which most foreigners favoured and enlisted with a small Left-Wing opposition group called the P.O.U.M. (*Partido Obrero de Unificacion Marxista*).

Orwell was in action and narrowly missed being killed. A stray bullet went through his neck, a millimetre from his wind-pipe and carotid artery. By the time he was out of hospital, the P.O.U.M. had been denounced by the Spanish Communists, probably at the instigation of Russia, and Orwell and his wife had to slip quietly out of the country to save their lives.

Orwell's experiences in Spain are recounted in his *Homage to Catalonia* (1938), praised by Tom Hopkinson as "a first-rate piece of reporting, vivid, dramatic, remorselessly objective". One of the episodes Orwell describes is how he was shot, included because "the whole experience of being hit by a bullet is very interesting and I think it is worth describing in detail". How typically Orwellian!

Among much poetry and prose that the Spanish war inspired, Orwell's book stands out as an honest record of a shameful struggle. The personal reminiscences more than compensate for two lengthy chapters which analyze a very involved and despicable political situation, and it is not surprising that *Homage to Catalonia* is still regarded as one of Orwell's best books.

Strangely enough, the grime of a dishonourable war, the treachery and savagery of the Communists, left him "with not less but more belief in the decency of human beings". This Spanish interlude was the second crisis of his adult life: so much of his writing after 1937 was political—a desperate concern to show his fellow-men the dangers of Communism, to expose the sores of social inequalities, to debunk the hollow promises and empty propaganda of politicians, including those of his own persuasion. As Wordsworth's faith in the French Revolution was shattered by the tyranny of Napoleon, so Orwell's hopes in the Russian Revolution were dashed by what he had witnessed in Spain.

When Orwell returned to England from Spain, except for a winter in Morocco he lived in Hertfordshire, writing, keeping hens and gardening; "outside my work," he once wrote, "the thing I care most about is gardening, especially vegetable gardening".

His fourth novel, *Coming up for Air* was published in 1939. It is the story of George Bowling, an ordinary, middle-aged, good-natured insurance salesman who revisits the scenes of his boyhood only to find them swamped by the flood of modern "improvements" and progress. Orwell had railed against the money god in *Keep the Aspidistra Flying*; now he turned to uncontrolled gimcrack building and industrial expansion, the rash of suburbia, the racket of the Building Societies, the fears of the average man, the dangers of the approaching war.

When war did break out, Orwell, as one would expect, tried to join the Forces. From childhood he had been ill with lung trouble and this weakness, and his Spanish war wound, kept him out of the Army. He was very disappointed; in 1940 he wrote: "My health is wretched, but it has never prevented me from doing anything I wanted to, except, so far, fight in the present war."

He joined the Home Guard—the Fireside Fusiliers he called them—and spent most of the war years overworking, mainly in the Indian service of the B.B.C. broadcasting to Malaya. It seems probable that only Japanese monitors heard his carefully prepared scripts, scripts that his friend and colleague Mr. Brander has called "a marvel of conciseness and clarity".

That Orwell's love of his fellow-men was no idle clap-trap is illustrated by the fact that he and his wife often went without their meagre wartime rations "so that there should be more for other people". Those who tried to exist on officially controlled rations during the 1939-45 war will realize what a sacrifice this was. It becomes even more saintly—I am sure that is the right word—when one realizes that it hastened the death of Mrs. Orwell who had not sufficient strength to recover from a minor operation in 1945.

That same year brought Orwell success as well as sorrow. He was writing regularly for a number of periodicals and newspapers, among them *Tribune* and the *Observer*, and for certain American journals. But much more important than even high-class journalism was the publication of *Animal Farm*, refused by four publishers and finally appearing at the best possible moment—the month the war with Germany ended and criticism of Russia was not frowned on as it had been some years before.

The animals of Manor Farm, urged on by Major, an old boar

who is dying, rebel against Mr. Jones, the drunken owner of the farm and take over control. Snowball and Napoleon, two pigs, rule tolerably well; an attack by Jones and his men is beaten off. But gradually power begins to corrupt the leaders of Animal Farm; Snowball, the more intelligent of the two, is deposed by Napoleon who uses brute force and systematic blackening of Snowball's character to make himself dictator over farm and animals. A well-intentioned rising for freedom ends in the stranglehold of slavery.

Animal Farm is a satire on Russian Stalinism, authoritarian government and human fallibility. The animals correspond to actual human beings or human types. For example, Snowball is a sly picture of Trotsky, Napoleon of Stalin; Squealer, appropriately named, is the modern propagandist, full of clever, convincing arguments. The farm has its OGPU, its Commissars, purges and forced confessions, false statistics and thuggery.

It was the first book in which Orwell had consciously tried "to fuse political and artistic purpose into one whole". Politically, it leaves totalitarianism looking like a sieve; artistically, it is satire at its most effective—pithy, humorous, controlled, purposeful, rapier-like, no strident hysteria, direct, capable of being read at several levels, its symbolism obvious but not blatant. Of all Orwell's books this is one that will live; it has often been compared with *Gulliver's Travels*, as its author has been likened to Swift, and one critic has called it "a work of genius in the lofty tradition of English humorous writing". It is only ninety pages long; I would recommend it as the first book a student of Orwell should read.

The publication of *Animal Farm* was not only Orwell's first financial success; it was also his first real contact with a wide, popular public. This fame was repeated when the posthumous television production of *1984* made Orwell's name temporarily as familiar as that of Gilbert Harding or Wilfred Pickles.

Journalism kept Orwell in London for two more years except for a tour of the ruined cities of Europe as war correspondent for the *Observer*. Then, in 1947, he suddenly left for Jura, a lonely Hebridean island off the west coast of Scotland, taking his adopted son with him. It was almost as if he had signed his own death warrant: the climate of Jura and the primitive conditions of life on an isolated farm, damp as a delta, were the worst possible for a consumptive, and we must look for some impelling reason for Orwell's decision.

Why, then, did Orwell go to Jura? Possibly to rest and find some relief from work and people; possibly to get himself and his son away from a future atomic war, as he himself suggested; more probably to find peace and time to write his next, most depressing and, as it turned out, last book. Ronald Rees thinks there was a strong Robinson Crusoe streak in his make-up which discovered in Jura the sheer joy of carpentry, boating, fishing and growing things.

In the end his illness won and in 1949 he went into a sanatorium in Gloucestershire. *1984* was published; "it wouldn't have been so gloomy," he said, "if I hadn't been so ill".

Like the other novels, it is a sermon rather than a piece of orthodox fiction, a sermon this time with a hell-fire message: nothing exists that cannot be destroyed by totalitarianism, not even the spirit of man itself. Since Orwell wrote *1984* the horrors of concentration camps, war-time tortures, brain-washing and other atrocities have been widely revealed: was Orwell so far wrong as some critics have suggested?

Think for a moment of what happened to Winston Smith, the leading character—he can hardly be called a hero—of *1984*. Half-way through the book he is convinced that "they" can make you say anything—*anything*—"but they can't make you believe it"; the human, inner heart remains impregnable. At the end of the book, after O'Brien's persuasive tortures and the final agonies of Room 101, he is ready to believe that two and two make five; his love for Julia and hers for him have withered to specks of dry dust. Winston is a walking shadow; all the sound and fury of his crusade against the Party have ended not in the glorious bang of revolution but in a silent whimper of complete acquiescence.

In 1949 Orwell married again; his wife was Sonia Brownell, an editorial assistant on *Horizon*, a literary periodical to which Orwell frequently contributed. Together he and his wife looked into the future: there was to be a book on Conrad, stories which explored human relationships.

But none of their plans was to mature. Arrangements were made to move Orwell to Switzerland for treatment, an air passage was booked and all was ready. On 23rd January, 1950, three days before the plane was due to leave, a sudden haemorrhage attacked Orwell and within a few minutes he was dead.

It would be unwise for me to forecast Orwell's position in the hierarchy of English writers; he is too much of our own day as yet and, in any case, my own enthusiasm for the man and his works colours any claims he might have. Much of his writing was ephemeral, the weekly and monthly stint of topical articles, reviews and political comment, some of it slick, unconvincing and dogmatic, some of it good enough to earn this tribute from George Woodcock: "Even his journalistic fragments, unimportant as they may be from any other point of view, are distinguished from the work of other journalists by their excellent style."

His novels, as novels, are poor relations alongside his other work and that of many of his contemporaries; Wyndham Lewis complained that he had never been so bored by any work of fiction as by *Coming up for Air*, and *Keep the Aspidistra Flying* was not far behind. If, heresy though it may be, we try to forget that Orwell's novels are novels and think of them as disguised autobiography, imaginative reporting, political and social documentaries, they can then be read, enjoyed and judged in a new light. So much of Orwell's writing is autobiographical and his life was so uncompromising a campaign for certain principles that it is not susprising to find something of him in all the leading characters of his novels, from Flory of *Burmese Days* to Smith of *1984*.

Orwell was a man who thought over his problems and those of other people with a keen and selfless determination to seek the truth, wherever it was to be found, however appalling it might be. None of us wants to believe in the nightmares of *1984*, but even allowing for his illness Orwell obviously thought that the world of Big Brother was more than mere fiction. When I first read *1984*, I happened also to be reading Victor Kravchenko's *I Chose Freedom* (Hale, 1947), the personal and political life of a Soviet official. The parallels between Orwell's imaginary world and Kravchenko's real world were much too close for comfort. We, or some future generation, may be faced with something like Orwell's "brave new world" unless justice and liberty are defended by word and deed with the same courageous disregard for personal considerations that Orwell showed.

1984 has been criticized for its lack of inventiveness, particularly in background. Surely one of the reasons for Orwell's use of a familiar setting, familiar, that is, to anyone who lived in a bombed city during the last war, is that he wanted to show how near to us the horrors of *1984* are; they are not the figments of a crazy novelist's imagination but the inevitable results of man's inhumanity to man. It is of interest to note that in 1927 the Russian writer, Zamyatin, published a novel called *We* which Christopher Hollis calls Orwell's *Holinshed*. Colin Wilson has gone so far as to say that Orwell drew so largely on *We* that *1984* would not have been published if a translation of the Russian book had been available.

"Our age," Bertrand Russell wrote in an article on Orwell, "is dominated by politics," an opinion with which Orwell would have whole-heartedly agreed. "Every line of serious work that I have written since 1936," he insisted, "has been written, directly or indirectly, *against* totalitarianism and *for* democratic socialism, as I understand it." Wyndham Lewis classifies Orwell as almost purely a political writer, a political novelist and a political essayist. Political, I suggest, because he knew that the handling or mishandling of power determines whether we have liberty and decency or whether we rush blindly towards *1984*.

Political action for Orwell had to be judged by its effect on people: he did not ask, "has production gone up?" or "have we maintained our international prestige?"; instead the old-fashioned question, "has this action made people any happier?" The morality of politics was his concern and he realized only too well how many crimes are committed in the name of political expediency. "Political necessities sometimes turn out to be political mistakes" might have been said by Orwell as well as by Shaw's Warwick in *St. Joan*, except that Orwell would have substituted "usually" for "sometimes".

Clear writing and clear thinking are impossible in a totalitarian state and Orwell constantly pleaded for people to recognize that there was a connexion, a very close connexion, between the decay of language and the stifling of freedom, that the immediate enemies of truthfulness are the Press Lords, the film magnates and the bureaucrats. What are many of our inane comic-strips, sex novelettes and sadistic crime stories but half-cousins to the prolefeed flooding from Pornosec in Minitrue's Fiction Department?

The writer cannot, Orwell thinks, be chained to any party: "to write in plain, vigorous language, one has to think fearlessly, and if one thinks fearlessly, one cannot be politically orthodox." Or again: "No one who feels deeply about literature, or even prefers good English to bad, can accept the discipline of a political party." He was fanatical in his warnings against Communism, energetically deploring the efforts of highbrow writers who tried to justify its teachings. Communism was not the only enemy. There was, too, the riddled target of capitalism, responsible for the conditions Orwell found in industrial Lancashire and causing, as he puts it in his introduction to *British Pamphleteers*, "the horrors of the Industrial Revolution, the destruction of one culture after another, the piling-up of millions of human beings in hideous ant-heaps of cities and, above all, the enslavement of the coloured races".

Orwell directed our thoughts towards much that was and still is wrong with society and politics, but seldom offered a solution: he was more of an iconoclast than a social architect. He was no dilettante; could anyone be, whose opinions were tempered by the garrets of Paris, the tramps' dormitories of England, the trench fighting of Spain, the hangings and cruelties of Burma? So many of us condemn the iniquity of wars, social injustice, the plight of the poor, the starvation of millions of people, and then sink back into a comfortable chair and watch the television with a secret feeling of relief that we need do nothing about them. Not Orwell. Personal suffering and personal identification were the only way for him, the only fuel to feed the fires of social reform that burned inside him. Our lack of action is in essence a lack of that decency and loyalty towards our fellow-men that time and time again finds a place in Orwell's writing. Perhaps reading him will rouse our consciences.

V. S. Pritchett, writing in the *New Statesman* immediately after Orwell's death, referred to his "guilty conscience", the guilty conscience of the educated and privileged man which "could be allayed only by taking upon itself the pain, the misery, the dinginess and the pathetic but hard vulgarities of a stale and hopeless period". Laurence Brander has expressed a similar idea in rather more theological terms; he suggests that Orwell's submission to the discipline of poverty was a kind of vicarious suffering, a "taking upon oneself a share of the burden of the sins of the world". Without knowing Orwell, it is impossible to comment on this theory; I have found no coherent evidence for it in Orwell's works, and I mention it as an attractive and plausible idea that Orwell's intimate friends might support or condemn. For Mr. Brander it is "the key to Orwell's conduct of life".

He did not accept the comforts and doctrines of religion, although he realized that the decline of Christianity in our country left a gap in national life. "The major problem of our time," he wrote in 1943, "is the decay of the belief in personal immortality." And, a year later: "I would say that the decay of belief in personal immortality has been as important as the rise of machine civilization. . . . I do not want the belief in life after death to return, and in any case it is not likely to return. What I do point out is that its disappearance has left a big hole and that we ought to take notice of that fact."

This lack of faith undoubtedly worried Orwell, as it must worry all men and women who have two thoughts to rub together. One wonders whether, like Dr. Joad, he might have found a religious faith late in life in spite of his conviction that for the majority of people religion was as dead as yesterday's pork chops. He was sure that a religious though not a strictly Christian attitude of life must be restored but "the only body of doctrine available to the Western world is one which the great mass of people are obviously less and less willing to accept". Christopher Hollis has tried to show how near to a religious view of life Orwell came; many of the questions he posed, suggests Mr. Hollis, are only soluble within a religious framework.

John Atkins in his book on Orwell (particularly useful for its relation of Orwell's journalism to his better-known books) states that "Orwell's uniqueness lay in his having the mind of an intellectual and the feelings of a common man". This dichotomy is behind much of his writing. On the one hand, he wrote mainly in the periodicals read by the intellectuals, trying to persuade his often sceptical audience of the validity of commonplace or popular opinion. Even at Crossgates this side of his personality had been obvious to Cyril Connolly: ". . . he alone among the boys was an intellectual, and not a parrot, for he thought for himself, read Shaw and Samuel Butler, and rejected not only St. Wulfric's, but the war, the Empire, Kipling, Sussex and Character."

On the other hand there was a trust in ordinary folk, their neighbourliness, their respect for each other, their inherent if often submerged will to see a way through complexities that baffle the intellectual. He saw the real issue of the Spanish war, of the 1939–45 war and perhaps of other wars yet to come as a fight for the common man to live a decent life. In Spain he genuinely felt that he had found, apart from an almost universal urge to steal, decent behaviour among the simple Catalans with whom he lived; here was the nearest he ever came to his ideal of a class-less, snob-less society. Happiness, he admitted after the last war, was not a normal condition among adult human beings, "but perhaps it *could* be made normal and it is upon this question that all serious political controversy really turns". We are, in fact, back again to Orwell's plea for brotherly love. Without a simple loyalty between human beings, chaos is inevitable: "either power politics must yield to common decency," he wrote in *Horizon* in 1943, "or the world must go spiralling down into a nightmare of which we can already catch some dim glimpses." A few years later Dachau and Buchenwald in fact, *1984* in fiction, turned these dim glimpses into startling realities; it is the proles of *1984* who retain their humanity, rough, coarse, stupid though they are; they alone in that ghastly world know happiness; in them alone lies hope.

Orwell's interest in the working classes, romantic and senti-mental though it may have been, was life-long. Before the age of six his heroes were fishermen, blacksmiths and bricklayers; the farm-labourers who gave him rides; the builders who let him play with mortar and taught him to swear; the plumber with whose children he went birdnesting. There is nothing extra-ordinary in this; it probably happens to the majority of children. But Crossgates, Eton and Burma failed to kill Orwell's interest. Even though there may be some truth in John Beavan's statement that Orwell never attained a deep understanding of the ordinary English wage-earner and his aspirations, he never ceased to champion the masses. For example, in his wartime diary on 3rd June, 1940, he noted that Lady Oxford had written in a letter to the *Daily Telegraph*: "since most London houses are deserted, there is little entertaining . . . in any case, most people have to part with their cooks and live in hotels". Orwell comments: "Apparently nothing will ever teach these people that the other ninety per cent of the population exist."

Finally, let me say a word or two about Orwell's much-praised prose style, a style that is as much part of his personality as any of the other characteristics I have been discussing: the style is indeed the man.

It is at its best in the essays, *Shooting an Elephant* for example; it is clear, unaffected, strong, economical and capable of being adapted to a variety of uses—exposition, description, argument, criticism. He was true to himself and it followed that there is no conscious falsity in what he wrote and how he wrote it. He himself believed that "the great enemy of clear language is insincerity" and one of his friends has claimed that the clarity of his style was the direct result of his genuine search for freedom. Sir Richard Rees goes to the very root of the matter in this tribute: "The secret of his prose style, which compared to most contemporary prose is like a clear running stream beside a tank of chemicals, is that its source is in a mind and heart of exceptional purity and nobility."

Orwell's own comment on a Ministry of Information pamphlet, *The Battle of Britain*, epitomizes his views on prose style. The pamphlet was marred, he felt, by its propagandist note and excessive use of such words as "heroic" and "glorious"; "why couldn't they simply give a cold, accurate account of the facts?" Virtually everything that Orwell wrote before 1940 was written at least twice, his books three times, individual passages as many as ten times. The deterioration after 1940 he attributed directly to the war and no doubt shed it along with his Home Guard uniform.

There is, of course, the black side to Orwell's writing. Like all journalists, he made blunders; like all men fired by enthusiasm, he misjudged and misrepresented, though probably not deliberately; like all human beings, he could be inconsistent and perverse.

An American reviewer of his *The Lion and the Unicorn* (1941) wrote: "he uses terms in a shockingly vague way; he makes sweeping generalizations with the confidence of ignorance; his innocence of scientific criteria is appalling".

Later in life, Orwell wrote and thought much about words— perhaps after reading the American reviews of *The Lion and the Unicorn*! The early books do not show that precision and care for *le mot juste* which dominate his prose style in, say, *Animal Farm*; only someone with an intense interest in language could have written the appendix to *1984* on "The Principles of Newspeak", the official language of Oceania. Even during his last illness, his interest did not flag: T. R. Fyvel found him reading the newspapers and carefully noting any instances of journalistic misuse of words.

Readers of Orwell will build up their own conception of the man and all he stood for. My own feeling about him, and the picture of him I like to keep in my mind, was expressed by Richard Peters in a broadcast two years ago: he described Orwell as "a lonely, courageous figure passing with detached honesty and without rancour across the mudbanks of corruption".

Keswick,
September 1957   G. B.

Shooting an Elephant

IN Moulmein, in Lower Burma, I was hated by large numbers of people—the only time in my life that I have been important enough for this to happen to me. I was sub-divisional police officer of the town, and in an aimless, petty kind of way anti-European feeling was very bitter. No one had the guts to raise a riot, but if a European woman went through the bazaars alone somebody would probably spit betel juice over her dress. As a police officer I was an obvious target and was baited whenever it seemed safe to do so. When a nimble Burman tripped me up on the football field and the referee (another Burman) looked the other way, the crowd yelled with hideous laughter. This happened more than once. In the end the sneering yellow faces of young men that met me everywhere, the insults hooted after me when I was at a safe distance, got badly on my nerves. The young Buddhist priests were the worst of all. There were several thousands of them in the town and none of them seemed to have anything to do except stand on street corners and jeer at Europeans.

All this was perplexing and upsetting. For at that time I had already made up my mind that imperialism was an evil thing and the sooner I chucked up my job and got out of it the better. Theoretically—and secretly, of course—I was all for the Burmese and all against their oppressors, the British. As for the job I was doing, I hated it more bitterly than I can perhaps make clear. In a job like that you see the dirty work of Empire at close quarters. The wretched prisoners huddling in the stinking cages of the lock-ups, the grey, cowed faces of the long-term convicts, the scarred buttocks of the men who had been flogged with bamboos—all these oppressed me with an intolerable sense of guilt. But I could get nothing into perspective. I was young and ill-educated and I had had to think out my problems in the utter silence that is imposed on every Englishman in the East. I did not even know that the British Empire is dying, still less did I know that it is a great deal better than the younger empires that are going to supplant it. All I knew was that I was stuck between my hatred of the empire I served and my rage against the evil-spirited little beasts who tried to make my job impossible. With one part of my mind I thought of the British Raj as an unbreakable tyranny, as something clamped down, in *sæcula sæculorum*, upon the will of prostrate peoples; with another part I thought that the greatest joy in the world would be to drive a bayonet into a Buddhist priest's guts. Feelings like these are the normal by-products of imperialism; ask any Anglo-Indian official, if you can catch him off duty.

One day something happened which in a roundabout way was enlightening. It was a tiny incident in itself, but it gave me a better glimpse than I had had before of the real nature of imperialism—the real motives for which despotic governments act. Early one morning the sub-inspector at a police station the other end of the town rang me up on the 'phone and said that an elephant was ravaging the bazaar. Would I please come and do something about it? I did not know what I could do, but I wanted to see what was happening and I got on to a pony and started out. I took my rifle, an old .44 Winchester and much too small to kill an elephant, but I thought the noise might be useful *in terrorem*. Various Burmans stopped me on the way and told me about the elephant's doings. It was not, of course, a wild elephant, but a tame one which had gone "must". It had been chained up, as tame elephants always are when their attack of "must" is due, but on the previous night it had broken its chain and escaped. Its mahout, the only person who could manage it when it was in that state, had set out in pursuit, but had taken the wrong direction and was now twelve hours' journey away, and in the morning the elephant had suddenly reappeared in the town. The Burmese population had no weapons and were quite helpless against it. It had already destroyed somebody's bamboo hut, killed a cow and raided some fruit-stalls and devoured the stock; also it had met the municipal rubbish van, and, when the driver jumped out and took to his heels, had turned the van over and inflicted violences upon it.

The Burmese sub-inspector and some Indian constables were waiting for me in the quarter where the elephant had been seen. It was a very poor quarter, a labyrinth of squalid bamboo huts, thatched with palm-leaf, winding all over a steep hillside. I remember that it was a cloudy, stuffy morning at the beginning of the rains. We began questioning the people as to where the elephant had gone, and, as usual, failed to get any definite information. That is invariably the case in the East; a story always sounds clear enough at a distance, but the nearer you get to the scene of events the vaguer it becomes. Some of the people said that the elephant had gone in one direction, some said that he had gone in another, some professed not even to have heard of any elephant. I had almost made up my mind that the whole story was a pack of lies, when we heard yells a little distance away. There was a loud, scandalized cry of "Go away, child! Go away this instant!" and an old woman with a switch in her hand came round the corner of a hut, violently shooing away a crowd of naked children. Some more women followed, clicking their tongues and exclaiming; evidently there was something that the children ought not to have seen. I rounded the hut and saw a man's dead body sprawling in the mud. He was an Indian, a black Dravidian coolie, almost naked, and he could not have been dead many minutes. The people said that the elephant had come suddenly upon him round the corner of the hut, caught him with its trunk, put its foot on his back and ground him into the earth. This was the rainy season and the ground was soft, and his face had scored a trench a foot deep and a couple of yards long. He was lying on his belly with his arms crucified and head sharply twisted to one side. His face was coated with mud, the eyes wide open, the teeth bared and grinning with an expression of unendurable agony. (Never tell me, by the way, that the dead look peaceful. Most of the corpses I have seen looked devilish.) The friction of the great beast's foot had stripped the skin from his back as neatly as one skins a rabbit. As soon as I saw the dead man I sent an orderly to a friend's house nearby to borrow an elephant rifle. I had already sent back the pony, not wanting it to go mad with fright and throw me if it smelt the elephant.

The orderly came back in a few minutes with a rifle and five cartridges, and meanwhile some Burmans had arrived and told us that the elephant was in the paddy fields below, only a few hundred yards away. As I started forward practically the whole population of the quarter flocked out of the houses and followed me. They had seen the rifle and were all shouting excitedly that I was going to shoot the elephant. They had not shown much interest in the elephant when he was merely ravaging their homes, but it was different now that he was going to be shot. It was a bit of fun to them, as it would be to an English crowd; besides they wanted the meat. It made me vaguely uneasy. I had no intention of shooting the elephant—I had merely sent for the rifle to defend myself if necessary—and it is always un-nerving to have a crowd following you. I marched down the hill, looking and feeling a fool, with the rifle over my shoulder and an ever-growing army of people jostling at my heels. At the bottom, when you got away from the huts, there was a metalled road and beyond that a miry waste of paddy fields a thousand yards across, not yet ploughed but soggy from the first rains and dotted with coarse grass. The elephant was standing eight yards from the road, his left side towards us. He took not the slightest notice of the crowd's approach. He was tearing up bunches of grass, beating them against his knees to clean them and stuffing them into his mouth.

I had halted on the road. As soon as I saw the elephant I knew with perfect certainty that I ought not to shoot him. It is a serious matter to shoot a working elephant—it is comparable to destroying a huge and costly piece of machinery—and obviously one ought not to do it if it can possibly be avoided. And at that distance, peacefully eating, the elephant looked no more dangerous than a cow. I thought then and I think now that his attack of "must" was already passing off; in which case he would merely wander harmlessly about until the mahout came back and caught him. Moreover, I did not in the least want to shoot him. I decided that I would watch him for a little while to make sure that he did not turn savage again, and then go home.

But at that moment I glanced round at the crowd that had followed me. It was an immense crowd, two thousand at the least and growing every minute. It blocked the road for a long distance on either side. I looked at the sea of yellow faces above the garish clothes—faces all happy and excited over this bit of fun, all certain that the elephant was going to be shot. They were watching me as they would watch a conjurer about to perform a trick. They did not like me, but with the magical rifle in my hands I was momentarily worth watching. And suddenly I realized that I should have to shoot the elephant after all. The people expected it of me and I had got to do it; I could feel their two thousand wills pressing me forward, irresistibly. And it was at this moment, as I stood there with the rifle in my hands, that I first grasped the hollowness, the futility of the white man's dominion in the East. Here was I, the white man with his gun, standing in front of the unarmed native crowd—seemingly the leading actor of the piece; but in reality I was only an absurd puppet pushed to and fro by the will of those yellow faces behind. I perceived in this moment that when the white man turns tyrant it is his own freedom that he destroys. He becomes a sort of hollow, posing dummy, the conventionalized figure of a sahib. For it is the condition of his rule that he shall spend his life in trying to impress the "natives", and so in every crisis he has got to do what the "natives" expect of him. He wears a mask, and his face grows to fit it. I had got to shoot the elephant. I had committed myself to doing it when I sent for the rifle. A sahib has got to act like a sahib; he has got to appear resolute, to know his own mind and do definite things. To come all that way, rifle in hand, with two thousand people marching at my heels, and then to trail feebly away, having done nothing —no, that was impossible. The crowd would laugh at me. And my whole life, every white man's life in the East, was one long struggle not to be laughed at.

But I did not want to shoot the elephant. I watched him beating his bunch of grass against his knees, with that preoccupied grandmotherly air that elephants have. It seemed to me that it would be murder to shoot him. At that age I was not squeamish about killing animals, but I had never shot an elephant and never wanted to. (Somehow it always seems worse to kill a *large* animal.) Besides, there was the beast's owner to be considered. Alive, the elephant was worth at least a hundred pounds; dead, he would only be worth the value of his tusks, five pounds, possibly. But I had got to act quickly. I turned to some experienced-looking Burmans who had been there when we arrived, and asked them how the elephant had been behaving. They all said the same thing: he took no notice of you if you left him alone, but he might charge if you went too close to him.

It was perfectly clear to me what I ought to do. I ought to walk up to within, say, twenty-five yards of the elephant and test his behaviour. If he charged I could shoot, if he took no notice of me it would be safe to leave him until the mahout came back. But also I knew that I was going to do no such thing. I was a poor shot with a rifle and the ground was soft mud into which one would sink at every step. If the elephant charged and I missed him, I should have about as much chance as a toad under a steam-roller. But even then I was not thinking particularly of my own skin, only of the watchful yellow faces behind. For at that moment, with the crowd watching me, I was not afraid in the ordinary sense, as I would have been if I had been alone. A white man mustn't be frightened in front of "natives"; and so, in general, he isn't frightened. The sole thought in my mind was that if anything went wrong those two thousand Burmans would see me pursued, caught, trampled on and reduced to a grinning corpse like that Indian up the hill. And if that happened it was quite probable that some of them would laugh. That would never do. There was only one alternative. I shoved the cartridges into the magazine and lay down on the road to get a better aim.

The crowd grew very still, and a deep, low, happy sigh, as of people who see the theatre curtain go up at last, breathed from innumerable throats. They were going to have their bit of fun after all. The rifle was a beautiful German thing with cross-hair sights. I did not then know that in shooting an elephant one would shoot to cut an imaginary bar running from ear-hole to ear-hole. I ought, therefore, as the elephant was sideways on, to have aimed straight at his ear-hole; actually I aimed several inches in front of this, thinking the brain would be further forward.

When I pulled the trigger I did not hear the bang or feel the kick—one never does when a shot goes home—but I heard the devilish roar of glee that went up from the crowd. In that instant, in too short a time, one would have thought, even for the bullet to get there, a mysterious, terrible change had come over the elephant. He neither stirred nor fell, but every line of his body had altered. He looked suddenly stricken, shrunken, immensely old, as though the frightful impact of the bullet had paralysed him without knocking him down. At last, after what seemed a long time—it might have been five seconds, I dare say—he sagged flabbily to his knees. His mouth slobbered. An enormous senility seemed to have settled upon him. One could have imagined him thousands of years old. I fired again into the same spot. At the second shot he did not collapse but climbed with desperate slowness to his feet and stood weakly upright, with legs sagging and head drooping. I fired a third time. That was the shot that did for him. You could see the agony of it jolt his whole body and knock the last remnant of strength from his legs. But in falling he seemed for a moment to rise, for as his hind legs collapsed beneath him he seemed to tower upwards like a huge rock toppling, his trunk reaching skywards like a tree. He trumpeted, for the first and only time. And then down he came, his belly towards me, with a crash that seemed to shake the ground even where I lay.

I got up. The Burmans were already racing past me across the mud. It was obvious that the elephant would never rise again, but he was not dead. He was breathing very rhythmically with long rattling gasps, his great mound of a side painfully rising and falling. His mouth was wide open—I could see far down into caverns of pale pink throat. I waited a long time for him to die, but his breathing did not weaken. Finally I fired my two remaining shots into the spot where I thought his heart must be. The thick blood welled out of him like red velvet, but still he did not die. His body did not even jerk when the shots hit him, the tortured breathing continued without a pause. He was dying, very slowly and in great agony, but in some world remote from me where not even a bullet could damage him further. I felt that I had got to put an end to that dreadful noise. It seemed dreadful to see the great beast lying there, powerless to move and yet powerless to die, and not even to be able to finish him. I sent back for my small rifle and poured shot after shot into his heart and down his throat. They seemed to make no impression. The tortured gasps continued as steadily as the ticking of a clock.

In the end I could not stand it any longer and went away. I heard later that it took him half an hour to die. Burmans were bringing dahs and baskets even before I left, and I was told they had stripped his body almost to the bones by the afternoon.

Afterwards, of course, there were endless discussions about the shooting of the elephant. The owner was furious, but he was only an Indian and could do nothing. Besides, I legally had done the right thing, for a mad elephant has to be killed, like a mad dog, if its owner fails to control it. Among the Europeans opinion was divided. The older men said I was right, the younger men said it was a damn shame to shoot an elephant for killing a coolie, because an elephant was worth more than any damn Coringhee coolie. And afterwards I was very glad that the coolie had been killed; it put me legally in the right and it gave me a sufficient pretext for shooting the elephant. I often wondered whether any of the others grasped that I had done it solely to avoid looking a fool.

1936.

Down the Mine

Our civilization, *pace* Chesterton, is founded on coal, more completely than one realizes until one stops to think about it. The machines that keep us alive, and the machines that make machines, are all directly or indirectly dependent upon coal. In the metabolism of the Western world the coal-miner is second in importance only to the man who ploughs the soil. He is a sort of caryatid upon whose shoulders nearly everything that is not grimy is supported. For this reason the actual process by which coal is extracted is well worth watching, if you get the chance and are willing to take the trouble.

When you go down a coal-mine it is important to try and get to the coal face when the "fillers" are at work. This is not easy, because when the mine is working visitors are a nuisance and are not encouraged, but if you go at any other time, it is possible to come away with a totally wrong impression. On a Sunday, for instance, a mine seems almost peaceful. The time to go there is when the machines are roaring and the air is black with coal dust, and when you can actually see what the miners have to do. At those times the place is like hell, or at any rate like my own mental picture of hell. Most of the things one imagines in hell are there—heat, noise, confusion, darkness, foul air, and, above all, unbearably cramped space. Everything except the fire, for there is no fire down there except the feeble beams of Davy lamps and electric torches which scarcely penetrate the clouds of coal dust.

When you have finally got there—and getting there is a job in itself: I will explain that in a moment—you crawl through the last line of pit props and see opposite you a shiny black wall three or four feet high. This is the coal face. Overhead is the smooth ceiling made by the rock from which the coal has been cut; underneath is the rock again, so that the gallery you are in is only as high as the ledge of coal itself, probably not much more than a yard. The first impression of all, overmastering everything else for a while, is the frightful, deafening din from the conveyor belt which carries the coal away. You cannot see very far, because the fog of coal dust throws back the beam of your lamp, but you can see on either side of you the line of half-naked kneeling men, one to every four or five yards, driving their shovels under the fallen coal and flinging it swiftly over their left shoulders. They are feeding it on to the conveyor belt, a moving rubber belt a couple of feet wide which runs a yard or two behind them. Down this belt a glittering river of coal races constantly. In a big mine it is carrying away several tons of coal every minute. It bears it off to some place in the main roads where it is shot into tubs holding half a ton, and thence dragged to the cages and hoisted to the outer air.

It is impossible to watch the "fillers" at work without feeling a pang of envy for their toughness. It is a dreadful job that they do, an almost superhuman job by the standards of an ordinary person. For they are not only shifting monstrous quantities of coal, they are also doing it in a position that doubles or trebles the work. They have got to remain kneeling all the while—they could hardly rise from their knees without hitting the ceiling—and you can easily see by trying it what a tremendous effort this means. Shovelling is comparatively easy when you are standing up, because you can use your knee and thigh to drive the shovel along; kneeling down, the whole of the strain is thrown upon your arm and belly muscles. And the other conditions do not exactly make things easier. There is the heat—it varies, but in some mines it is suffocating—and the coal dust that stuffs up your throat and nostrils and collects along your eyelids, and the unending rattle of the conveyor belt, which in that confined space is rather like the rattle of a machine gun. But the fillers look and work as though they were made of iron. They really do look like iron—hammered iron statues—under the smooth coat of coal dust which clings to them from head to foot. It is only when you see miners down the mine and naked that you realize what splendid men they are. Most of them are small (big men are at a disadvantage in that job) but nearly all of them have the most noble bodies; wide shoulders tapering to slender supple waists, and small pronounced buttocks and sinewy thighs, with not an ounce of waste flesh anywhere. In the hotter mines they wear only a pair of thin drawers, clogs and knee-pads; in the hottest mines of all, only the clogs and knee-pads. You can hardly tell by the look of them whether they are young or old. They may be any age up to sixty or even sixty-five, but when they are black and naked they all look alike. No one could do their work who had not a young man's body, and a figure fit for a guardsman at that; just a few pounds of extra flesh on the waist-line, and the constant bending would be impossible. You can never forget that spectacle once you have seen it—the line of bowed, kneeling figures, sooty black all over, driving their huge shovels under the coal with stupendous force and speed. They are on the job for seven and a half hours, theoretically without a break, for there is no time "off". Actually they snatch a quarter of an hour or so at some time during the shift to eat the food they have brought with them, usually a hunk of bread and dripping and a bottle of cold tea. The first time I was watching the "fillers" at work I put my hand upon some dreadful slimy thing among the coal dust. It was a chewed quid of tobacco. Nearly all the miners chew tobacco, which is said to be good against thirst.

Probably you have to go down several coal-mines before you can get much grasp of the processes that are going on round you. This is chiefly because the mere effort of getting from place to place makes it difficult to notice anything else. In some ways it is even disappointing, or at least is unlike what you have expected. You get into the cage, which is a steel box about as wide as a telephone box and two or three times as long. It holds ten men, but they pack it like pilchards in a tin, and a tall man cannot stand upright in it. The steel door shuts upon you, and somebody working the winding gear above drops you into the void.

You have the usual momentary qualm in your belly and a bursting sensation in the ears, but not much sensation of movement till you get near the bottom, when the cage slows down so abruptly that you could swear it is going upwards again. In the middle of the run the cage probably touches sixty miles an hour; in some of the deeper mines it touches even more. When you crawl out at the bottom you are perhaps four hundred yards underground. That is to say you have a tolerable-sized mountain on top of you; hundreds of yards of solid rock, bones of extinct beasts, subsoil, flints, roots of growing things, green grass and cows grazing on it—all this suspended over your head and held back only by wooden props as thick as the calf of your leg. But because of the speed at which the cage has brought you down, and the complete blackness through which you have travelled, you hardly feel yourself deeper down than you would at the bottom of the Piccadilly tube.

What *is* surprising, on the other hand, is the immense horizontal distances that have to be travelled underground. Before I had been down a mine I had vaguely imagined the miner stepping out of the cage and getting to work on a ledge of coal a few yards away. I had not realized that before he even gets to his work he may have had to creep along passages as long as from London Bridge to Oxford Circus. In the beginning, of course, a mine shaft is sunk somewhere near a seam of coal. But as that seam is worked out and fresh seams are followed up, the workings get further and further from the pit bottom. If it is a mile from the pit bottom to the coal face, that is probably an average distance; three miles is a fairly normal one; there are even said to be a few mines where it is as much as five miles. But these distances bear no relation to distances above ground. For in all that mile or three miles as it may be, there is hardly anywhere outside the main road, and not many places even there, where a man can stand upright.

You do not notice the effect of this till you have gone a few hundred yards. You start off, stooping slightly, down the dim-lit gallery, eight or ten feet wide and about five high, with the walls built up with slabs of shale, like the stone walls in Derbyshire. Every yard or two there are wooden props holding up the beams and girders; some of the girders have buckled into fantastic curves under which you have to duck. Usually it is bad going underfoot—thick dust or jagged chunks of shale, and in some mines where there is water it is as mucky as a farm-yard. Also there is the track for the coal tubs, like a miniature railway track with sleepers a foot or two apart, which is tiresome to walk on. Everything is grey with shale dust; there is a dusty fiery smell which seems to be the same in all mines. You see mysterious machines of which you never learn the purpose, and bundles of tools slung together on wires, and sometimes mice darting away from the beam of the lamps. They are surprisingly common, especially in mines where there are or have been horses. It would be interesting to know how they got there in the first place; possibly by falling down the shaft—for they say a mouse can fall any distance uninjured, owing to its surface area being so large relative to its weight. You press yourself against the wall to make way for lines of tubs jolting slowly towards the shaft, drawn by an endless steel cable operated from the surface. You creep through sacking curtains and thick wooden doors which, when they are opened, let out fierce blasts of air. These doors are an important part of the ventilation system. The exhausted air is sucked out of one shaft by means of fans, and the fresh air enters the other of its own accord. But if left to itself the air will take the shortest way round, leaving the deeper workings un-ventilated; so all the short cuts have to be partitioned off.

At the start to walk stooping is rather a joke, but it is a joke that soon wears off. I am handicapped by being exceptionally tall, but when the roof falls to four feet or less it is a tough job for anybody except a dwarf or a child. You not only have to bend double, you have also got to keep your head up all the while so as to see the beams and girders and dodge them when they come. You have, therefore, a constant crick in the neck, but this is nothing to the pain in your knees and thighs. After half a mile it becomes (I am not exaggerating) an unbearable agony. You begin to wonder whether you will ever get to the end—still more, how on earth you are going to get back. Your pace grows slower and slower. You come to a stretch of a couple of hundred yards where it is all exceptionally low and you have to work yourself along in a squatting position. Then suddenly the roof opens out to a mysterious height—scene of an old fall of rock, probably—and for twenty whole yards you can stand upright. The relief is overwhelming. But after this there is another low stretch of a hundred yards and then a succession of beams which you have to crawl under. You go down on all fours; even this is a relief after the squatting business. But when you come to the end of the beams and try to get up again, you find that your knees have temporarily struck work and refuse to lift you. You call a halt, ignominiously, and say that you would like to rest for a minute or two. Your guide (a miner) is sympathetic. He knows that your muscles are not the same as his. "Only another four hundred yards," he says encouragingly; you feel that he might as well say another four hundred miles. But finally you do somehow creep as far as the coal face. You have gone a mile and taken the best part of an hour; a miner would do it in not much more than twenty minutes. Having got there, you have to sprawl in the coal dust and get your strength back for several minutes before you can even watch the work in progress with any kind of intelligence.

Coming back is worse than going, not only because you are already tired out but because the journey back to the shaft is slightly uphill. You get through the low places at the speed of a tortoise, and you have no shame now about calling a halt when your knees give way. Even the lamp you are carrying becomes a nuisance and probably when you stumble you drop it; whereupon, if it is a Davy lamp, it goes out. Ducking the beams becomes more and more of an effort, and sometimes you forget to duck. You try walking head down as the miners do, and then you bang your backbone. Even the miners bang their backbones fairly often. This is the reason why in very hot mines, where it is necessary to go about half naked, most of the miners have what they call "buttons down the back"—that is, a permanent scab on each vertebra. When the track is downhill the miners sometimes fit their clogs, which are hollow underneath, on to the trolley rails and slide down. In mines where the "travelling" is very bad all the miners carry sticks about two and a half feet long, hollowed out below the handle. In normal places you keep your hand on top of the stick and in the low places you slide your hand down into the hollow. These sticks are a great help, and the wooden crash-helmets—a comparatively recent invention— are a godsend. They look like a French or Italian steel helmet, but they are made of some kind of pith and very light, and so strong that you can take a violent blow on the head without feeling it. When finally you get back to the surface you have been perhaps three hours underground and travelled two miles, and you are more exhausted than you would be by a twenty-five-mile walk above ground. For a week afterwards your thighs are so stiff that coming downstairs is quite a difficult feat; you have to work your way down in a peculiar sidelong manner, without bending the knees. Your miner friends notice the stiffness of your walk and chaff you about it. ("How'd ta like to work down pit, eh?" etc.) Yet even a miner who has been long away from work—from illness, for instance—when he comes back to the pit, suffers badly for the first few days.

It may seem that I am exaggerating, though no one who has been down an old-fashioned pit (most of the pits in England are old-fashioned) and actually gone as far as the coal face, is likely to say so. But what I want to emphasize is this. Here is this frightful business of crawling to and fro, which to any normal person is a hard day's work in itself; and it is not part of the miner's work at all, it is merely an extra, like the City man's daily ride in the Tube. The miner does that journey to and fro, and sandwiched in between there are seven and a half hours of savage work. I have never travelled much more than a mile to the coal face; but often it is three miles, in which case I and most people other than coal-miners would never get there at all. This is the kind of point that one is always liable to miss. When you think of the coal-mine you think of depth, heat, darkness, blackened figures hacking at walls of coal; you don't think, necessarily, of those miles of creeping to and fro. There is the question of time, also. A miner's working shift of seven and a half hours does not sound very long, but one has got to add on to it at least an hour a day for "travelling", more often two hours and sometimes three. Of course, the "travelling" is not technically work and the miner is not paid for it; but it is as like work as makes no difference. It is easy to say that miners don't mind all this. Certainly, it is not the same for them as it would be for you or me. They have done it since childhood, they have the right muscles hardened, and they can move to and fro underground with a startling and rather horrible agility. A miner puts his head down and runs, with a long swinging stride, through places where I can only stagger. At the workings you see them on all fours, skipping round the pit props almost like dogs. But it is quite a mistake to think that they enjoy it. I have talked about this to scores of miners and they all admit that the "travelling" is hard work; in any case when you hear them discussing a pit among themselves the "travelling" is always one of the things they discuss. It is said that a shift always returns from work faster than it goes; nevertheless the miners all say that it is the coming away after a hard day's work, that is especially irksome. It is part of their work and they are equal to it, but certainly it is an effort. It is comparable, perhaps to climbing a smallish mountain before and after your day's work.

When you have been down in two or three pits you begin to get some grasp of the processes that are going on underground. (I ought to say, by the way, that I know nothing whatever about the technical side of mining: I am merely describing what I have seen.) Coal lies in thin seams between enormous layers

of rock, so that essentially the process of getting it out is like
scooping the central layer from a Neapolitan ice. In the old days
the miners used to cut straight into the coal with pick and
crowbar—a very slow job because coal, when lying in its virgin
state, is almost as hard as rock. Nowadays the preliminary work
is done by an electrically-driven coal-cutter, which in principle
is an immensely tough and powerful band-saw, running horizon-
tally instead of vertically, with teeth a couple of inches long and
half an inch or an inch thick. It can move backwards or forwards
on its own power, and the men operating it can rotate it this
way or that. Incidentally it makes one of the most awful noises
I have ever heard, and sends forth clouds of coal dust which
make it impossible to see more than two to three feet and almost
impossible to breathe. The machine travels along the coal face
cutting into the base of the coal and undermining it to the depth
of five feet or five feet and a half; after it is comparatively easy to
extract the coal to the depth to which it has been undermined.
Where it is "difficult getting", however, it has also to be loosened
with explosives. A man with an electric drill, like a rather small
version of the drills used in street-mending, bores holes at
intervals in the coal, inserts blasting powder, plugs it with clay,
goes round the corner if there is one handy (he is supposed to
retire to twenty-five yards distance) and touches off the charge
with an electric current. This is not intended to bring the coal
out, only to loosen it. Occasionally, of course, the charge is too
powerful, and then it not only brings the coal out but brings
the roof down as well.

After the blasting has been done the "fillers" can tumble the
coal out, break it up and shovel it on to the conveyor belt. It
comes out first in monstrous boulders which may weigh anything
up to twenty tons. The conveyor belt shoots it on to tubs, and
the tubs are shoved into the main road and hitched on to an
endlessly revolving steel cable which drags them to the cage.
Then they are hoisted, and at the surface the coal is sorted by
being run over screens, and if necessary is washed as well. As

far as possible the "dirt"—the shale, that is—is used for making the roads below. All that cannot be used is sent to the surface and dumped; hence the monstrous "dirt-heaps", like hideous grey mountains, which are the characteristic scenery of the coal areas. When the coal has been extracted to the depth to which the machine has cut, the coal face has advanced by five feet. Fresh props are put in to hold up the newly exposed roof, and during the next shift the conveyor belt is taken to pieces, moved five feet forward and re-assembled. As far as possible the three operations of cutting, blasting and extraction are done in three separate shifts, the cutting in the afternoon, the blasting at night (there is a law, not always kept, that forbids its being done when other men are working near by), and the "filling" in the morning shift, which lasts from six in the morning until half-past one.

Even when you watch the process of coal-extraction you probably only watch it for a short time, and it is not until you begin making a few calculations that you realize what a stupendous task the "fillers" are performing. Normally each man has to clear a space four or five yards wide. The cutter has undermined the coal to the depth of five feet, so that if the seam of coal is three or four feet high, each man has to cut out, break up and load on to the belt something between seven and twelve cubic yards of coal. This is to say, taking a cubic yard as weighing twenty-seven hundred-weight, that each man is shifting coal at a speed approaching two tons an hour. I have just enough experience of pick and shovel work to be able to grasp what this means. When I am digging trenches in my garden, if I shift two tons of earth during the afternoon, I feel that I have earned my tea. But earth is tractable stuff compared with coal, and I don't have to work kneeling down, a thousand feet underground, in suffocating heat and swallowing coal dust with every breath I take; nor do I have to walk a mile bent double before I begin. The miner's job would be as much beyond my power as it would be to perform on a flying trapeze or to win the Grand National. I am not a manual labourer and please God I never shall be one, but there are some kinds of manual work that I could do if I had to. At a pitch I could be a tolerable road-sweeper or an inefficient gardener or even a tenth-rate farm hand. But by no conceivable amount of effort or training could I become a coal-miner; the work would kill me in a few weeks.

Watching coal-miners at work, you realize momentarily what different universes people inhabit. Down there where coal is dug is a sort of world apart which one can quite easily go through life without ever hearing about. Probably a majority of people would even prefer not to hear about it. Yet it is the absolutely necessary counterpart of our world above. Practically everything we do, from eating an ice to crossing the Atlantic, and from baking a loaf to writing a novel, involves the use of coal, directly or indirectly. For all the arts of peace coal is needed; if war breaks out it is needed all the more. In time of revolution the miner must go on working or the revolution must stop, for revolution as much as reaction needs coal. Whatever may be happening on the surface, the hacking and shovelling have got to continue without a pause, or at any rate without pausing for more than a few weeks at the most. In order that Hitler may march the goose-step, that the Pope may denounce Bolshevism, that the cricket crowds may assemble at Lord's, that the poets may scratch one another's backs, coal has got to be forthcoming. But on the whole we are not aware of it; we all know that we "must have coal", but we seldom or never remember what coal-getting involves. Here am I sitting writing in front of my comfortable coal fire. It is April but I still need a fire. Once a fortnight the coal cart drives up to the door and men in leather jerkins carry the coal indoors in stout sacks smelling of tar and shoot it clanking into the coal-hole under the stairs. It is only very rarely, when I make a definite mental effort, that I connect this coal with that far-off labour in the mines. It is just "coal"— something that I have got to have; black stuff that arrives mysteriously from nowhere in particular, like manna except that you have to pay for it. You could quite easily drive a car right across the north of England and never once remember that hundreds of feet below the road you are on the miners are hacking at the coal. Yet in a sense it is the miners who are driving your car forward. Their lamp-lit world down there is as necessary to the daylight world above as the root is to the flower.

It is not long since conditions in the mines were worse than they are now. There are still living a few very old women who in their youth have worked underground, with the harness round their waists, and a chain that passed between their legs, crawling on all fours and dragging tubs of coal. They used to go on doing this even when they were pregnant. And even now, if coal could not be produced without pregnant women dragging it to and fro, I fancy we should let them do it rather than deprive ourselves of coal. But most of the time, of course, we should prefer to forget that they were doing it. It is so with all types of manual work; it keeps us alive, and we are oblivious of its existence. More than anyone else, perhaps, the miner can stand as the type of the manual worker, not only because his work is so exaggeratedly awful, but also because it is so vitally necessary and yet so remote from our experience, so invisible, as it were, that we are capable of forgetting it as we forget the blood in our veins. In a way it is even humiliating to watch coal-miners working. It raises in you a momentary doubt about your own status as an "intellectual" and a superior person generally. For it is brought home to you, at least while you are watching, that it is only because miners sweat their guts out that superior persons can remain superior. You and I and the editor of the *Times Lit. Supp.*, and the poets and the Archbishop of Canterbury and Comrade X, author of *Marxism for Infants*—all of us *really* owe the comparative decency of our lives to poor drudges underground, blackened to the eyes, with their throats full of coal dust, driving their shovels forward with arms and belly muscles of steel.

1937.

Skirmish in Spain

ONE afternoon Benjamin told us that he wanted fifteen volunteers. The attack on the Fascist redoubt which had been called off on the previous occasion was to be carried out to-night. I oiled my ten Mexican cartridges, dirtied my bayonet (the things give your position away if they flash too much), and packed up a hunk of bread, three inches of red sausage, and a cigar which my wife had sent from Barcelona and which I had been hoarding for a long time. Bombs were served out, three to a man. The Spanish Government had at last succeeded in producing a decent bomb. It was on the principle of a Mills bomb, but with two pins instead of one. After you had pulled the pins out there was an interval of seven seconds before the bomb exploded. Its chief disadvantage was that one pin was very stiff and the other very loose, so that you had the choice of leaving both pins in place and being unable to pull the stiff one out in a moment of emergency, or pulling out the stiff one beforehand and being in a constant stew lest the thing should explode in your pocket. But it was a handy little bomb to throw.

A little before midnight Benjamin led the fifteen of us down to Torre Fabian. Ever since evening the rain had been pelting down. The irrigation ditches were brimming over, and every time you stumbled into one you were in water up to your waist. In the pitch darkness and sheeting rain in the farm-yard a dim mass of men was waiting. Kopp addressed us, first in Spanish, then in English, and explained the plan of attack. The Fascist line here made an L-bend and the parapet we were to attack lay on rising ground at the corner of the L. About thirty of us, half English, and half Spanish, under the command of Jorge Roca, our battalion commander (a battalion in the militia was about four hundred men), and Benjamin, were to creep up and cut the Fascist wire. Jorge would fling the first bomb as a signal, then the rest of us were to send in a rain of bombs, drive the Fascists out of the parapet and seize it before they could rally. Simultaneously seventy Shock Troopers were to assault the next Fascist "position", which lay two hundred yards to the right of the other, joined to it by a communication-trench. To prevent us from shooting each other in the darkness white armlets would be worn. At this moment a messenger arrived to say that there were no white armlets. Out of the darkness a plaintive voice suggested: "Couldn't we arrange for the Fascists to wear white armlets instead?"

There was an hour or two to put in. The barn over the mule stable was so wrecked by shell-fire that you could not move about in it without a light. Half the floor had been torn away by a plunging shell and there was a twenty-foot drop on to the stones beneath. Someone found a pick and levered a burst plank out of the floor, and in a few minutes we had got a fire alight and our drenched clothes were steaming. Someone else produced a pack of cards. A rumour—one of those mysterious rumours that are endemic in war—flew round that hot coffee with brandy in it was about to be served out. We filed eagerly down the almost-collapsing staircase and wandered round the dark yard, enquiring where the coffee was to be found. Alas! there was no coffee. Instead, they called us together, ranged us into single file, and then Jorge and Benjamin set off rapidly into the darkness, the rest of us following.

It was still raining and intensely dark, but the wind had dropped. The mud was unspeakable. The paths through the beet-fields were simply a succession of lumps, as slippery as a greasy pole, with huge pools everywhere. Long before we got to the place where we were to leave our own parapet everyone had fallen several times and our rifles were coated with mud. At the parapet a small knot of men, our reserves, were waiting, and the doctor and a row of stretchers. We filed through the gap in the parapet and waded through another irrigation ditch. Splash-gurgle! Once again in water up to your waist, with the filthy, slimy mud oozing over your boot-tops. On the grass outside Jorge waited till we were all through. Then, bent almost double, he began creeping slowly forward. The Fascist parapet was about a hundred and fifty yards away. Our one chance of getting there was to move without noise.

I was in front with Jorge and Benjamin. Bent double, but with faces raised, we crept into the almost utter darkness at a pace that grew slower at every step. The rain beat lightly in our faces. When I glanced back I could see the men who were nearest to me, a bunch of humped shapes like huge black mushrooms gliding slowly forward. But every time I raised my head Benjamin, close beside me, whispered fiercely in my ear: "To keep ze head down! To keep ze head down!" I could have told him that he needn't worry. I knew by experiment that on a dark night you can never see a man at twenty paces. It was far more important to go quietly. If they once heard us we were done for. They had only to spray the darkness with their machine-gun and there was nothing for it but to run or be massacred.

But on the sodden ground it was almost impossible to move quietly. Do what you would your feet stuck to the mud, and every step you took was slop-slop, slop-slop. And the devil of it was that the wind had dropped, and in spite of the rain it was a very quiet night. Sounds would carry a long way. There was a dreadful moment when I kicked against a tin and thought every Fascist within miles must have heard it. But no, not a sound, no answering shot, no movement in the Fascist lines. We crept onwards, always more slowly. I cannot convey to you the depth of my desire to get there. Just to get within bombing distance before they heard us! At such a time you have not even any fear, only a tremendous hopeless longing to get over the intervening ground. I have felt exactly the same thing when stalking a wild animal; the same agonized desire to get within range, the same dreamlike certainty that it is impossible. And how the distance stretched out! I knew the ground well, it was barely a hundred and fifty yards, and yet it seemed more like a mile. When you are creeping at that pace you are aware as an ant might be of the enormous variations in the ground; the splendid patch of smooth grass here, the evil patch of sticky mud there, the tall rustling reeds that have got to be avoided, the heap of stones that almost makes you give up hope because it seems impossible to get over it without noise.

We had been creeping forward for such an age that I began to think we had gone the wrong way. Then in the darkness thin parallel lines of something blacker were faintly visible. It was the outer wire (the Fascists had two lines of wire). Jorge knelt down, fumbled in his pocket. He had our only pair of wire-cutters. Snip, snip. The trailing stuff was lifted delicately aside. We waited for the men at the back to close up. They seemed to be making a frightful noise. It might be fifty yards to the Fascist parapet now. Still onwards, bent double. A stealthy step, lowering your foot as gently as a cat approaching a mousehole; then a pause to listen; then another step. Once I raised my head; in silence Benjamin put his hand behind my neck and pulled it violently down. I knew that the inner wire was barely twenty yards from the parapet. It seemed to me inconceivable that thirty men could get there unheard. Our breathing was enough to give us away. Yet somehow we did get there. The Fascist parapet was visible now, a dim black mound, looming high above us. Once again Jorge knelt and fumbled. Snip, snip. There was no way of cutting the stuff silently.

So that was the inner wire. We crawled through it on all fours and rather more rapidly. If we had time to deploy now all was well. Jorge and Benjamin crawled across to the right. But the men behind, who were spread out, had to form into single file to get through the narrow gap in the wire, and just at this moment there was a flash and a bang from the Fascist parapet. The sentry had heard us at last. Jorge poised himself on one knee and swung his arm like a bowler. Crash! His bomb burst some-where over the parapet. At once, far more promptly than one would have thought possible, a roar of fire, ten or twenty rifles,

burst out from the Fascist parapet. They had been waiting for
us after all. Momentarily you could see every sand-bag in the
lurid light. Men too far back were flinging their bombs and
some of them were falling short of the parapet. Every loophole
seemed to be spouting jets of flame. It is always hateful to be
shot at in the dark—every rifle-flash seems to be pointed straight
at yourself—but it was the bombs that were the worst. You
cannot conceive the horror of these things till you have seen
one burst close to you and in darkness; in the daytime there is
only the crash of the explosion, in the darkness there is the
blinding red glare as well. I had flung myself down at the first
volley. All this while I was lying on my side in the greasy mud,
wrestling savagely with the pin of a bomb. The damned thing
would not come out. Finally I realized that I was twisting it in
the wrong direction. I got the pin out, rose to my knees, hurled
the bomb, and threw myself down again. The bomb burst over
to the right, outside the parapet; fright had spoiled my aim.
Just at this moment another bomb burst right in front of me,
so close that I could feel the heat of the explosion. I flattened
myself out and dug my face into the mud so hard that I hurt my
neck and thought that I was wounded. Through the din I
heard an English voice behind me say quietly: "I'm hit." The
bomb had, in fact, wounded several people round about me
without touching myself. I rose to my knees and flung my
second bomb. I forget where that one went.

The Fascists were firing, our people behind were firing, and I
was very conscious of being in the middle. I felt the blast of a
shot and realized that a man was firing from immediately behind
me. I stood up and shouted at him: "Don't shoot at me, you
bloody fool!" At this moment I saw that Benjamin, ten or
fifteen yards to my right, was motioning to me with his arm.
I ran across to him. It meant crossing the line of spouting loop-
holes, and as I went I clapped my left hand over my cheek; an
idiotic gesture—as though one's hand could stop a bullet!—but
I had a horror of being hit in the face. Benjamin was kneeling

on one knee with a pleased, devilish sort of expression on his face and firing carefully at the rifle-flashes with his automatic pistol. Jorge had dropped wounded at the first volley and was somewhere out of sight. I knelt beside Benjamin, pulled the pin out of my third bomb and flung it. Ah! No doubt about it that time. The bomb crashed inside the parapet, at the corner, just by the machine-gun nest.

The Fascist fire seemed to have slackened very suddenly. Benjamin leapt to his feet and shouted: "Forward! Charge!" We dashed up the short steep slope on which the parapet stood. I say "dashed"; "lumbered" would be a better word; the fact is that you can't move fast when you are sodden and mudded from head to foot and weighted down with a heavy rifle and bayonet and a hundred and fifty cartridges. I took it for granted that there would be a Fascist waiting for me at the top. If he fired at that range he could not miss me, and yet somehow I never expected him to fire, only to try for me with his bayonet. I seemed to feel in advance the sensation of our bayonets crossing, and I wondered whether his arm would be stronger than mine. However, there was no Fascist waiting. With a vague feeling of relief I found that it was a low parapet and the sand-bags gave a good foothold. As a rule they are difficult to get over. Everything inside was smashed to pieces, beams flung all over the place, and great shards of uralite littered everywhere. Our bombs had wrecked all the huts and dug-outs. And still there was not a soul visible. I thought they would be lurking somewhere underground, and shouted in English (I could not think of any Spanish at the moment): "Come on out of it! Surrender!" No answer. Then a man, a shadowy figure in the half-light, skipped over the roof of one of the ruined huts and dashed away to the left. I started after him, prodding my bayonet ineffectually into the darkness. As I rounded the corner of the hut I saw a man—I don't know whether or not it was the same man as I had seen before—fleeing up the communication-trench that led to the other Fascist position. I must have been very close to him, for

I could see him clearly. He was bareheaded and seemed to have nothing on except a blanket which he was clutching round his shoulders. If I had fired I could have blown him to pieces. But for fear of shooting one another we had been ordered to use only bayonets once we were inside the parapet, and in any case I never even thought of firing. Instead, my mind leapt backwards twenty years, to our boxing instructor at school, showing me in vivid pantomime how he had bayoneted a Turk at the Dardanelles. I gripped my rifle by the small of the butt and lunged at the man's back. He was just out of my reach. Another lunge: still out of reach. And for a little distance we proceeded like this, he rushing up the trench and I after him on the ground above, prodding at his shoulder-blades and never quite getting there—a comic memory for me to look back upon, though I suppose it seemed less comic to him.

Of course, he knew the ground better than I and had soon slipped away from me. When I came back the position was full of shouting men. The noise of firing had lessened somewhat. The Fascists were still pouring a heavy fire at us from three sides, but it was coming from a greater distance. We had driven them back for the time being. I remember saying in an oracular manner: "We can hold this place for half an hour, not more." I don't know why I picked on half an hour. Looking over the right-hand parapet you could see innumerable greenish rifle-flashes stabbing the darkness; but they were a long way back, a hundred or two hundred yards. Our job now was to search the position and loot anything that was worth looting. Benjamin and some others were already scrabbling among the ruins of a big hut or dug-out in the middle of the position. Benjamin staggered excitedly through the ruined roof, tugging at the rope handle of an ammunition box.

"Comrades! Ammunition! Plenty ammunition here!"

"We don't want ammunition," said a voice, "we want rifles."

This was true. Half our rifles were jammed with mud and unusable. They could be cleaned, but it is dangerous to take

the bolt out of a rifle in the darkness; you put it down somewhere and then you lose it. I had a tiny electric torch which my
wife had managed to buy in Barcelona, otherwise we had no
light of any description between us. A few men with good
rifles began a desultory fire at the flashes in the distance. No
one dared fire too rapidly; even the best of the rifles were liable
to jam if they got too hot. There were about sixteen of us inside
the parapet, including one or two who were wounded. A number
of wounded, English and Spanish, were lying outside. Patrick
O'Hara, a Belfast Irishman who had had some training in first-aid,
went to and fro with packets of bandages, binding up the wounded
men and, of course, being shot at every time he returned to the
parapet, in spite of his indignant shouts of "Poum!"

We began searching the position. There were several dead
men lying about, but I did not stop to examine them. The thing
I was after was the machine-gun. All the while when we were
lying outside I had been wondering vaguely why the gun did
not fire. I flashed my torch inside the machine-gun nest. A
bitter disappointment! The gun was not there. Its tripod was
there, and various boxes of ammunition and spare parts, but the
gun was gone. They must have unscrewed it and carried it off
at the first alarm. No doubt they were acting under orders, but
it was a stupid and cowardly thing to do, for if they had kept
the gun in place they could have slaughtered the whole lot
of us. We were furious. We had set our hearts on capturing a
machine-gun.

We poked here and there but did not find anything of much
value. There were quantities of Fascist bombs lying about—a
rather inferior type of bomb, which you touched off by pulling
a string—and I put a couple of them in my pocket as souvenirs,
It was impossible not to be struck by the bare misery of the
Fascist dug-outs. The litter of spare clothes, books, food, petty
personal belongings that you saw in our own dug-outs was
completely absent; these poor unpaid conscripts seemed to own
nothing except blankets and a few soggy hunks of bread. Up at

the far end there was a small dug-out which was partly above ground and had a tiny window. We flashed the torch through the window and instantly raised a cheer. A cylindrical object in a leather case, four feet high and six inches in diameter, was leaning against the wall. Obviously the machine-gun barrel. We dashed round and got in at the doorway, to find that the thing in the leather case was not a machine-gun but something which, in our weapon-starved army, was even more precious. It was an enormous telescope, probably of at least sixty or seventy magnifications, with a folding tripod. Such telescopes simply did not exist on our side of the line and they were desperately needed. We brought it out in triumph and leaned it against the parapet, to be carried off later.

At this moment someone shouted that the Fascists were closing in. Certainly the din of firing had grown very much louder. But it was obvious that the Fascists would not counter-attack from the right, which meant crossing no man's land and assaulting their own parapet. If they had any sense at all they would come at us from inside the line. I went round to the other side of the dug-outs. The position was roughly horse-shoe-shaped, with the dug-outs in the middle, so that we had another parapet covering us on the left. A heavy fire was coming from that direction, but it did not matter greatly. The danger-spot was straight in front, where there was no protection at all. A stream of bullets was passing just overhead. They must be coming from the other Fascist position farther up the line; evidently the Shock Troopers had not captured it after all. But this time the noise was deafening. It was the unbroken, drum-like roar of massed rifles which I was used to hearing from a little distance; this was the first time I had been in the middle of it. And by now, of course, the firing had spread along the line for miles around. Douglas Thompson, with a wounded arm dangling useless at his side, was leaning against the parapet and firing one-handed at the flashes. Someone whose rifle had jammed was loading for him.

There were four or five of us round this side. It was obvious
what we must do. We must drag the sand-bags from the front
parapet and make a barricade across the unprotected side. And
we had got to be quick. The fire was high at present, but they
might lower it at any moment; by the flashes all round I could
see that we had a hundred or two hundred men against us. We
began wrenching the sand-bags loose, carrying them twenty
yards forward and dumping them into a rough heap. It was a
vile job. They were big sand-bags, weighing a hundredweight
each and it took every ounce of your strength to prise them loose;
and then the rotten sacking split and the damp earth cascaded
all over you, down your neck and up your sleeves. I remember
feeling a deep horror at everything: the chaos, the darkness, the
frightful din, the slithering to and fro in the mud, the struggles
with the bursting sand-bags—all the time encumbered with my
rifle, which I dared not put down for fear of losing it. I even
shouted to someone as we staggered along with a bag between
us: "This is war! Isn't it bloody?" Suddenly a succession of tall
figures came leaping over the front parapet. As they came nearer
we saw that they wore the uniform of the Shock Troopers, and
we cheered, thinking they were reinforcements. However, there
were only four of them, three Germans and a Spaniard. We
heard afterwards what had happened to the Shock Troopers.
They did not know the ground and in the darkness had been led
to the wrong place, where they were caught on the Fascist wire
and numbers of them were shot down. These were four who
had got lost, luckily for themselves. The Germans did not speak
a word of English, French or Spanish. With difficulty and much
gesticulation we explained what we were doing and got them to
help us in building the barricade.

The Fascists had brought up a machine-gun now. You could
see it spitting like a squib a hundred or two hundred yards away;
the bullets came over us with a steady, frosty crackle. Before long
we had flung enough sand-bags into place to make a low breast-
work behind which the few men who were on this side of the

position could lie down and fire. I was kneeling behind them.
A mortar-shell whizzed over and crashed somewhere in no man's
land. That was another danger, but it would take them some
minutes to find our range. Now that we had finished wrestling
with those beastly sand-bags it was not bad fun in a way; the
noise, the darkness, the flashes approaching, our own men
blazing back at the flashes. One even had time to think a little.
I remember wondering whether I was frightened, and deciding
that I was not. Outside, where I was probably in less danger, I
had been half sick with fright. Suddenly there was another shout
that the Fascists were closing in. There was no doubt about it
this time, the rifle-flashes were much nearer. I saw a flash hardly
twenty yards away. Obviously they were working their way up
the communication-trench. At twenty yards they were within
easy bombing range; there were eight or nine of us bunched
together and a single well-placed bomb would blow us all to
fragments. Bob Smillie, the blood running down his face from
a small wound, sprang to his knee and flung a bomb. We cowered,
waiting for the crash. The fuse fizzled red as it sailed through the
air, but the bomb failed to explode. (At least a quarter of these
bombs were duds.) I had no bombs left except the Fascist ones
and I was not certain how these worked. I shouted to the others
to know if anyone had a bomb to spare. Douglas Moyle felt in
his pocket and passed one across. I flung it and threw myself on
my face. By one of those strokes of luck that happen about once
in a year I had managed to drop the bomb almost exactly where
the rifle had flashed. There was the roar of the explosion and
then, instantly, a diabolical outcry of screams and groans. We
had got one of them, anyway; I don't know whether he was
killed, but certainly he was badly hurt. Poor wretch, poor
wretch! I felt a vague sorrow as I heard him screaming. But at
the same instant, in the dim light of the rifle-flashes, I saw or
thought I saw a figure standing near the place where the rifle
had flashed. I threw up my rifle and let fly. Another scream,
but I think it was still the effect of the bomb. Several more

bombs were thrown. The next rifle-flashes we saw were a long way off, a hundred yards or more. So we had driven them back, temporarily at least.

Everyone began cursing and saying why the hell didn't they send us some supports. With a sub-machine-gun or twenty men with clean rifles we could hold this place against a battalion. At this moment Paddy Donovan, who was second-in-command to Benjamin and had been sent back for orders, climbed over the front parapet.

"Hi! Come on out of it! All men to retire at once!"

"What?"

"Retire! Get out of it!"

"Why?"

"Orders. Back to our own lines double-quick."

People were already climbing over the front parapet. Several of them were struggling with a heavy ammunition box. My mind flew to the telescope which I had left leaning against the parapet on the other side of the position. But at this moment I saw that the four Shock Troopers, acting I suppose on some mysterious orders they had received beforehand, had begun running up the communication-trench. It led to the other Fascist position and—if they got there—to certain death. They were disappearing into the darkness. I ran after them, trying to think of the Spanish for "retire"; finally I shouted, "Atras! Atras!" which perhaps conveyed the right meaning. The Spaniard understood it and brought the others back. Paddy was waiting at the parapet.

"Come on, hurry up."

"But the telescope!"

"B—— the telescope! Benjamin's waiting outside."

We climbed out. Paddy held the wire aside for me. As soon as we got away from the shelter of the Fascist parapet we were under a devilish fire that seemed to be coming at us from every direction. Part of it, I do not doubt, came from our own side, for everyone was firing all along the line. Whichever way we turned a fresh stream of bullets swept past; we were driven this

way and that in the darkness like a flock of sheep. It did not
make it any easier that we were dragging a captured box of
ammunition—one of those boxes that hold 1750 rounds and
weigh about a hundredweight—besides a box of bombs and
several Fascist rifles. In a few minutes, although the distance
from parapet to parapet was not two hundred yards and most
of us knew the ground, we were completely lost. We found
ourselves slithering about in a muddy field, knowing nothing
except that bullets were coming from both sides. There was no
moon to go by, but the sky was growing a little lighter. Our lines
lay east of Huesca; I wanted to stay where we were till the first
crack of dawn showed us which was east and which was west;
but the others were against it. We slithered onwards, changing
our direction several times and taking it in turns to haul at the
ammunition-box. At last we saw the low flat line of a parapet
looming in front of us. It might be ours or it might be the
Fascists'; nobody had the dimmest idea which way we were
going. Benjamin crawled on his belly through some tall whitish
weed till he was about twenty yards from the parapet and tried
a challenge. A shout of "Poum!" answered him. We jumped to
our feet, found our way along the parapet, slopped once more
through the irrigation ditch—splash-gurgle!—and were in
safety.

Kopp was waiting inside the parapet with a few Spaniards.
The doctor and the stretchers were gone. It appeared that all
the wounded had been got in except Jorge and one of our own
men, Hiddlestone by name, who were missing. Kopp was pacing
up and down, very pale. Even the fat folds at the back of his
neck were pale; he was paying no attention to the bullets that
streamed over the low parapet and cracked close to his head.
Most of us were squatting behind the parapet for cover. Kopp
was muttering. "Jorge! Cogno! Jorge!" And then in English. "If
Jorge is gone it is terreeble, terreeble!" Jorge was his personal
friend and one of his best officers. Suddenly he turned to us and
asked for five volunteers, two English and three Spanish, to go

and look for the missing men. Moyle and I volunteered with three Spaniards.

As we got outside the Spaniards murmured that it was getting dangerously light. This was true enough; the sky was dimly blue. There was a tremendous noise of excited voices coming from the Fascist redoubt. Evidently they had reoccupied the place in much greater force than before. We were sixty or seventy yards from the parapet when they must have seen or heard us, for they sent over a heavy burst of fire which made us drop on our faces. One of them flung a bomb over the parapet—a sure sign of panic. We were lying in the grass, waiting for an opportunity to move on, when we either heard or thought we heard— I have no doubt it was pure imagination, but it seemed real enough at the time—that the Fascist voices were much closer. They had left the parapet and were coming after us. "Run!" I yelled to Moyle, and jumped to my feet. And heavens, how I ran! I had thought earlier in the night that you can't run when you are sodden from head to foot and weighted down with a rifle and cartridges; I learned now you can *always* run when you think you have fifty or a hundred armed men after you. But if I could run fast, others could run faster. In my flight something that might have been a shower of meteors sped past me. It was the three Spaniards, who had been in front. They were back to our own parapet before they stopped and I could catch up with them. The truth was that our nerves were all to pieces. I knew, however, that in a half-light one man is invisible where five are clearly visible, so I went back alone. I managed to get to the outer wire and searched the ground as well as I could, which was not very well, for I had to lie on my belly. There was no sign of Jorge or Hiddlestone, so I crept back. We learned afterwards that both Jorge and Hiddlestone had been taken to the dressing-station earlier. Jorge was lightly wounded through the shoulder. Hiddlestone had received a dreadful wound—a bullet which travelled right up his left arm, breaking the bone in several places; as he lay helpless on the ground a bomb had burst near him and torn various other parts of his body. He recovered, I am glad to say. Later he told me that he had worked his way some distance lying on his back, then had clutched hold of a wounded Spaniard and they had helped one another in.

It was getting light now. Along the line for miles around a ragged meaningless fire was thundering, like the rain that goes on raining after a storm. I remember the desolate look of every-thing, the morasses of mud, the weeping poplar trees, the yellow water in the trench-bottoms; and men's exhausted faces, un-shaven, streaked with mud and blackened to the eyes with smoke. When I got back to my dug-out the three men I shared it with were already fast asleep. They had flung themselves down with all their equipment on and their muddy rifles clutched against them. Everything was sodden, inside the dug-out as well as outside. By long searching I managed to collect enough chips of dry wood to make a tiny fire. Then I smoked the cigar which I had been hoarding and which, surprisingly enough, had not got broken during the night.

Afterwards we learned that the action had been a success, as such things go. It was merely a raid to make the Fascists divert troops from the other side of Huesca, where the Anarchists were attacking again. I had judged that the Fascists had thrown a hundred or two hundred men into the counter-attack, but a deserter told us later on that it was six hundred. I dare say he was lying—deserters, for obvious reasons, often try to curry favour. It was a great pity about the telescope. The thought of losing that beautiful bit of loot worries me even now.

1938.

Marrakech

As the corpse went past the flies left the restaurant table in a cloud and rushed after it, but they came back a few minutes later.

The little crowd of mourners—all men and boys, no women—threaded their way across the market-place between the piles of pomegranates and the taxis and the camels, wailing a short chant over and over again. What really appeals to the flies is that the corpses here are never put into coffins, they are merely wrapped in a piece of rag and carried on a rough wooden bier on the shoulders of four friends. When the friends get to the burying-ground they hack an oblong hole a foot or two deep, dump the body in it and fling over it a little of the dried-up, lumpy earth, which is like broken brick. No gravestone, no name, no identifying mark of any kind. The burying-ground is merely a huge waste of hummocky earth, like a derelict building-lot. After a month or two no one can even be certain where his own relatives are buried.

When you walk through a town like this—two hundred thousand inhabitants, of whom at least twenty thousand own literally nothing except the rags they stand up in—when you see how the people live, and still more easily they die, it is always difficult to believe that you are walking among human beings. All colonial empires are in reality founded upon that fact. The people all have brown faces—besides, there are so many of them Are they really the same flesh as yourself? Do they even have names? Or are they merely a kind of undifferentiated brown stuff, about as individual as bees or coral insects? They rise out of the earth, they sweat and starve for a few years, and then they sink back into the nameless mounds of the graveyard and nobody notices that they are gone. And even the graves themselves soon fade back into the soil. Sometimes, out for a walk, as you break your way through the prickly pear, you notice that it is rather bumpy underfoot, and only a certain regularity in the bumps tells you that you are walking over skeletons.

I was feeding one of the gazelles in the public gardens.

Gazelles are almost the only animals that look good to eat when they are still alive; in fact, one can hardly look at their hindquarters without thinking of mint sauce. The gazelle I was feeding seemed to know that this thought was in my mind, for though it took the piece of bread I was holding out it obviously did not like me. It nibbled rapidly at the bread, then lowered its head and tried to butt me, then took another nibble and then butted again. Probably its idea was that if it could drive me away the bread would somehow remain hanging in mid-air.

An Arab navvy working on the path near by lowered his heavy hoe and sidled slowly towards us. He looked from the gazelle to the bread and from the bread to the gazelle, with a sort of quiet amazement, as though he had never seen anything quite like this before. Finally he said shyly in French:

"*I* could eat some of that bread."

I tore off a piece and he stowed it gratefully in some secret place under his rags. This man is an employee of the Municipality.

When you go through the Jewish quarters you gather some idea of what the medieval ghettoes were probably like. Under their Moorish rulers the Jews were only allowed to own land in certain restricted areas, and after centuries of this kind of treatment they have ceased to bother about overcrowding. Many of the streets are a good deal less than six feet wide, the houses are completely windowless, and sore-eyed children cluster everywhere in unbelievable numbers, like clouds of flies. Down the centre of the street there is generally running a little river of urine.

In the bazaar huge families of Jews, all dressed in the long black robe and little black skull-cap, are working in dark fly-infested booths that look like caves. A carpenter sits crosslegged at a prehistoric lathe, turning chair-legs at lightning speed. He works the lathe with a· bow in his right hand and guides the chisel with his left foot, and thanks to a lifetime of sitting in this position his left leg is warped out of shape. At his side his grandson, aged six, is already starting on the simpler parts of the job.

I was just passing the coppersmiths' booths when somebody noticed that I was lighting a cigarette. Instantly, from the dark holes all round, there was a frenzied rush of Jews, many of them old grandfathers with flowing grey beards, all clamouring for a cigarette. Even a blind man somewhere at the back of one of the booths heard a rumour of cigarettes and came crawling out, groping in the air with his hand. In about a minute I had used up the whole packet. None of these people, I suppose, works less than twelve hours a day, and every one of them looks on a cigarette as a more or less impossible luxury.

As the Jews live in self-contained communities they follow the same trades as the Arabs, except for agriculture. Fruit-sellers, potters, silversmiths, blacksmiths, butchers, leatherworkers, tailors, water-carriers, beggars, porters—whichever way you look you see nothing but Jews. As a matter of fact there are thirteen thousand of them, all living in the space of a few acres. A good job Hitler wasn't here. Perhaps he was on his way, however. You hear the usual dark rumours about the Jews, not only from the Arabs but from the poorer Europeans.

"Yes, *mon vieux*, they took my job away from me and gave it to a Jew. The Jews! They're the real rulers of this country, you know. They've got all the money. They control the banks, finance—everything."

"But," I said, "isn't it a fact that the average Jew is a labourer working for about a penny an hour?"

"Ah, that's only for show! They're all moneylenders really. They're cunning, the Jews."

In just the same way, a couple of hundred years ago, poor old women used to be burned for witchcraft when they could not even work enough magic to get themselves a square meal.

All people who work with their hands are partly invisible, and the more important the work they do, the less visible they are. Still, a white skin is always fairly conspicuous. In northern Europe, when you see a labourer ploughing a field, you probably give him a second glance. In a hot country, anywhere south of Gibraltar or east of Suez, the chances are that you don't even see him. I have noticed this again and again. In a tropical landscape one's eyes take in everything except the human beings. It takes in the dried-up soil, the prickly pear, the palm tree and the distant mountain, but it always misses the peasant hoeing at his patch. He is the same colour as the earth, and a great deal less interesting to look at.

It is only because of this that the starved countries of Asia and Africa are accepted as tourist resorts. No one would think of running cheap trips to the Distressed Areas. But where the human beings have brown skins their poverty is simply not noticed. What does Morocco mean to a Frenchman? An orange-grove or a job in Government service. Or to an Englishman? Camels, castles, palm trees, Foreign Legionnaires, brass trays and bandits. One could probably live there for years without noticing that for nine-tenths of the people the reality of life is an endless, back-breaking struggle to wring a little food out of an eroded soil.

Most of Morocco is so desolate that no wild animal bigger than a hare can live on it. Huge areas which were once covered with forest have turned into a treeless waste where the soil is exactly like broken-up brick. Nevertheless a good deal of it is cultivated, with frightful labour. Everything is done by hand. Long lines of women, bent double like inverted capital L's work their way slowly across the fields, tearing up the prickly weeds with their hands, and the peasant gathering lucerne for fodder pulls it up stalk by stalk instead of reaping it, thus saving an inch or two on each stalk. The plough is a wretched wooden thing, so frail that one can easily carry it on one's shoulder, and fitted underneath with a rough iron spike which stirs the soil to a depth of about four inches. This is as much as the strength of the animals is equal to. It is usual to plough with a cow and a donkey yoked together. Two donkeys would not be quite strong enough, but on the other hand two cows would cost a little more to feed. The peasants possess no harrows, they merely plough the soil several times over in different directions, finally leaving it in rough furrows, after which the whole field has to be shaped with hoes into small oblong patches to conserve water. Except for a day or two after the rare rainstorms there is never enough water. Along the edges of the fields channels are hacked out to a depth of thirty or forty feet to get at the tiny trickles which run through the subsoil.

Every afternoon a file of very old women passes down the road outside my house, each carrying a load of firewood. All of them are mummified with age and the sun, and all of them are tiny. It seems to be generally the case in primitive communities that the women, when they get beyond a certain age, shrink to the size of children. One day a poor old creature who could not have been more than four feet tall crept past me under a vast load of wood. I stopped her and put a five-sou piece (a little more than a farthing) into her hand. She answered with a shrill wail, almost a scream, which was partly gratitude but mainly surprise. I suppose that from her point of view, by taking any notice of her, I seemed almost to be violating a law of nature. She accepted her status as an old woman, that is to say as a beast of burden. When a family is travelling it is quite usual to see a father and a grown-up son riding ahead on donkeys, and an old woman following on foot, carrying the baggage.

But what is strange about these people is their invisibility. For several weeks, always at about the same time of day, the file of old women had hobbled past the house with their firewood, and though they had registered themselves on my eyeballs I cannot truly say that I had seen them. Firewood was passing—that was how I saw it. It was only that one day I happened to be walking behind them, and the curious up-and-down motion of a load of wood drew my attention to the human being beneath it. Then for the first time I noticed the poor old earth-coloured bodies, bodies reduced to bones and leathery skin, bent double under the crushing weight. Yet I suppose I had not been five minutes on Moroccan soil before I noticed the overloading of the donkeys and was infuriated by it. There is no question that the donkeys are damnably treated. The Moroccan donkey is hardly bigger than a St. Bernard dog, it carries a load which in the British Army would be considered too much for a fifteen-hands mule, and very often its pack-saddle is not taken off its back for weeks together. But what is peculiarly pitiful is that it is the most willing creature on earth, it follows its master like a dog and does not need either bridle or halter. After a dozen years of devoted work it suddenly drops dead, whereupon its master tips it into the ditch and the village dogs have torn its guts out before it is cold.

This kind of thing makes one's blood boil, whereas—on the whole—the plight of the human beings does not. I am not commenting, merely pointing to a fact. People with brown skins are next door to invisible. Anyone can be sorry for the donkey with its galled back, but it is generally owing to some kind of accident if one even notices the old woman under her load of sticks.

As the storks flew northward the Negroes were marching southward—a long, dusty column, infantry, screw-gun batteries, and then more infantry, four or five thousand men in all, winding up the road with a clumping of boots and a clatter of iron wheels.

They were Senegalese, the blackest Negroes in Africa, so black that sometimes it is difficult to see whereabouts on their necks the hair begins. Their splendid bodies were hidden in reach-me-down khaki uniforms, their feet squashed into boots that looked like blocks of wood, and every tin hat seemed to be a couple of sizes too small. It was very hot and the men had marched a long way. They slumped under the weight of their packs and the curiously sensitive black faces were glistening with sweat.

As they went past a tall, very young Negro turned and caught my eye. But the look he gave me was not in the least the kind of look you might expect. Not hostile, not contemptuous, not sullen, not even inquisitive. It was the shy, wide-eyed Negro look, which actually is a look of profound respect. I saw how it was. This wretched boy, who is a French citizen and has therefore been dragged from the forest to scrub floors and catch syphilis in garrison towns, actually has feelings of reverence before a white skin. He has been taught that the white race are his masters, and he still believes it.

But there is one thought which every white man (and in this connexion it doesn't matter twopence if he calls himself a socialist) thinks when he sees a black army marching past. "How much longer can we go on kidding these people? How long before they turn their guns in the other direction?"

It was curious, really. Every white man there had this thought stowed somewhere or other in his mind. I had it, so had the other onlookers, so had the officers on their sweating chargers and the white N.C.Os. marching in the ranks. It was a kind of secret which we all knew and were too clever to tell; only the Negroes didn't know it. And really it was like watching a flock of cattle to see the long column, a mile or two miles of armed men, flowing peacefully up the road, while the great white birds drifted over them in the opposite direction, glittering like scraps of paper.

                                                              1939.

The English Class System

In time of war the English class system is the enemy propagandist's best argument. To Dr. Goebbels's charge that England is still "two nations", the only truthful answer would have been that she is in fact three nations. But the peculiarity of English class distinctions is not that they are unjust—for after all, wealth and poverty exist side by side in almost all countries—but that they are anachronistic. They do not exactly correspond to economic distinctions, and what is essentially an industrial and capitalist country is haunted by the ghost of a caste system.

It is usual to classify modern society under three headings: the upper class or *bourgeoisie*, the middle class, or *petite bourgeoisie*, and the working class, or proletariat. This roughly fits the facts, but one can draw no useful inference from it unless one takes account of the subdivisions within the various classes and realizes how deeply the whole English outlook is coloured by romanticism and sheer snobbishness.

England is one of the last remaining countries to cling to the outward forms of feudalism. Titles are maintained and new ones are constantly created, and the House of Lords, consisting mainly of hereditary peers, has real powers. At the same time England has no real aristocracy. The race difference on which aristocratic rule is usually founded was disappearing by the end of the Middle Ages, and the famous medieval families have almost completely vanished. The so-called old families are those that grew rich in the sixteenth, seventeenth and eighteenth centuries. Moreover, the notion that nobility exists in its own right, that you can be a nobleman even if you are poor, was already dying out in the age of Elizabeth, a fact commented on by Shakespeare. And yet, curiously enough, the English ruling class has never developed into a *bourgeoisie* plain and simple. It has never become purely urban or frankly commercial. The ambition to be a country gentleman, to own and administer land and draw at least a part of your income from rent, has survived every change. So it comes that each new wave of parvenus, instead of simply replacing the existing ruling class, has adopted its habits, intermarried with it, and, after a generation or two, become indistinguishable from it.

The basic reason for this may perhaps be that England is very small and has an equable climate and pleasantly varied scenery. It is almost impossible in England, and not easy even in Scotland, to be more than twenty miles from a town. Rural life is less inherently boorish than it is in bigger countries with colder winters. And the comparative integrity of the British ruling class—for when all is said and done they have not behaved so contemptibly as their European opposite numbers—is probably bound up with their idea of themselves as feudal landowners. This outlook is shared by considerable sections of the middle class. Nearly everyone who can afford to do so sets up as a country gentleman, or at least makes some effort in that direction. The manor-house with its park and its walled gardens reappears in reduced form in the stockbroker's week-end cottage, in the suburban villa with its lawn and herbaceous border, perhaps even in the potted nasturtiums on the window-sill of the Bayswater flat. This wide-spread day-dream is undoubtedly snobbish, it has tended to stabilize class distinctions and has helped to prevent the modernization of English agriculture: but it is mixed up with a kind of idealism, a feeling that style and tradition are more important than money.

Within the middle class there is a sharp division, cultural and not financial, between those who aim at gentility and those who do not. According to the usual classification, everyone between the capitalist and the weekly wage-earner can be lumped together as "*petite bourgeoisie*". This means that the Harley Street physician, the army officer, the grocer, the farmer, the senior civil servant, the solicitor, the clergyman, the schoolmaster, the bank manager, the speculative builder, and the fisherman who owns his own boat, are all in the same class. But no one in England feels them to belong to the same class, and the distinction between them is not a distinction of income but of accent, manners and, to some extent, outlook. Anyone who pays any attention to class differences at all would regard an army officer with £1000 a year as socially superior to a shopkeeper with £2000 a year. Even within the upper class a similar distinction holds good, the titled person being almost always more deferred to than an untitled person of larger income. Middle-class people are really graded according to their degree of resemblance to the aristocracy: professional men, senior officials, officers in the fighting services, university lecturers, clergymen, even the literary and scientific intelligentsia, rank higher than business men, though on the whole they earn less. It is a peculiarity of this class that their largest item of expenditure is education. Whereas a successful tradesman will send his son to the local grammar school, a clergyman with half his income will underfeed himself for years in order to send his son to a public school, although he knows that he will get no direct return for the money he spends.

There is, however, another noticeable division in the middle class. The old distinction was between the man who is "a gentleman" and the man who is "not a gentleman". In the last thirty years, however, the demands of modern industry, and the technical schools and provincial universities, have brought into being a new kind of man, middle class in income and to some extent in habits, but not much interested in his own social status. People like radio engineers and industrial chemists, whose education has not been of a kind to give them any reverence for the past, and who tend to live in blocks of flats or housing-estates where the old social pattern has broken down, are the most nearly classless beings that England possesses. They are an important section of society, because their numbers are constantly growing. The war, for instance, made necessary the formation of an enormous air force, and so you got thousands of young men of working-class origin graduating into the technical middle class by way of the R.A.F. Any serious reorganization of industry now will have similar effects. And the characteristic outlook of the technicians is already spreading among the older strata of the middle class. One symptom of this is that intermarriage within the middle class is freer than it used to be. Another is the increasing unwillingness of people below the £2000 a year level to bankrupt themselves in the name of education.

Another series of changes, probably dating from the Education Bill of 1871, is occurring in the working class. One cannot altogether acquit the English working class either of snobbishness or of servility. To begin with there is a fairly sharp distinction between the better-paid working class and the very poor. Even in socialist literature it is common to find contemptuous references to slum-dwellers (the German word *lumpenproletariat* is much used), and imported labourers with low standards of living, such as the Irish, are greatly looked down on. There is also, probably, more disposition to accept class distinctions as permanent, and even to accept the upper classes as natural leaders, than survives in most countries. It is significant that in the moment of disaster the man best able to unite the nation was Churchill, a Conservative of aristocratic origins. The word "Sir" is much used in England, and the man of obviously upper-class appearance can usually get more than his fair share of deference from commissionaires, ticket-collectors, policemen and the like. It is this aspect of English life that seems most shocking to visitors from America and the Dominions. And the tendency towards servility probably did not decrease in the twenty years between the two wars: it may even have increased, owing chiefly to unemployment.

But snobbishness is never quite separable from idealism. The tendency to give the upper classes more than their due is mixed up with a respect for good manners and something vaguely describable as culture. In the South of England, at any rate, it is unquestionable that most working-class people want to resemble the upper classes in manners and habits. The traditional attitude of looking down on the upper classes as effeminate and "la-di-dah" survives best in the heavy-industry areas. Hostile nicknames like "toff" and "swell" have almost disappeared, and even the *Daily Worker* displays advertisements for "High-class Gentleman's Tailor". Above all, throughout southern England there is almost general uneasiness about the Cockney accent. In Scotland and northern England snobbishness about the local accents does exist, but it is not nearly so strong or widespread. Many a Yorkshireman definitely prides himself on his broad U's and narrow A's, and will defend them on linguistic grounds. In London there are still people who say "fice" instead of "face", but there is probably no one who regards "fice" as superior. Even a person who claims to despise the *bourgeoisie* and all its ways will still take care that his children grow up pronouncing their aitches.

But side by side with this there has gone a considerable growth of political consciousness and an increasing impatience with class privilege. Over a period of twenty or thirty years the working class has grown politically more hostile to the upper class, culturally less hostile. There is nothing incongruous in this: both tendencies are symptoms of the levelling of manners which results from machine civilization and which makes the English class system more and more of an anachronism.

The obvious class differences still surviving in England astonish foreign observers, but they are far less marked, and far less real, than they were thirty years ago. People of different social origins, thrown together during the war in the armed forces, or in factories or offices, or as firewatchers and Home Guards, were able to mingle more easily than they did in the 1914–18 war. It is worth listing the various influences which—mechanically, as it were—tend to make Englishmen of all classes less and less different from one another.

First of all, the improvement in industrial technique. Every year less and less people are engaged in heavy manual labour which keeps them constantly tied and, by hypertrophying certain muscles, gives them a distinctive carriage. Secondly, improvements in housing. Between the two wars rehousing was done mostly by the local authorities, who have produced a type of house (the council house, with its bathroom, garden, separate kitchen and indoor w.c.) which is nearer to the stockbroker's villa than it is to the labourer's cottage. Thirdly, the mass production of furniture which in ordinary times can be bought on the hire-purchase system. The effect of this is that the interior of a working-class house resembles that of a middle-class house very much more than it did a generation ago. Fourthly, and perhaps most important of all, the mass production of cheap clothes. Thirty years ago the social status of nearly everyone in England could be determined from his appearance, even at two hundred yards' distance. The working classes all wore ready-made clothes, and the ready-made clothes were not only ill-fitting but usually followed the upper-class fashions of ten or fifteen years earlier. The cloth cap was practically a badge of status. It was universal among the working class, while the upper classes only wore it for golf and shooting. This state of affairs is rapidly changing. Ready-made clothes now follow the fashions closely, they are made in many different fittings to suit every kind of figure, and even when they are of very cheap cloth they are superficially not very different from expensive clothes. The result is that it grows harder every year, especially in the case of women, to determine social status at a glance.

Mass-produced literature and amusements have the same effect. Radio programmes, for instance, are necessarily the same for everybody. Films, though often extremely reactionary in their implied outlook, have to appeal to a public of millions and therefore have to avoid stirring up class antagonisms. So also with some of the big-circulation newspapers. The *Daily Express*, for instance, draws its readers from all strata of the population. So also with some of the periodicals that have appeared in the past dozen years. *Punch* is obviously a middle- and upper-class paper, but *Picture Post* is not aimed at any particular class. And lending libraries and very cheap books, such as the Penguins, popularize the habit of reading and probably have a levelling effect on literary taste. Even taste in food tends to grow more uniform owing to the multiplication of cheap but fairly smart restaurants such as those of Messrs. Lyons.

We are not justified in assuming that class distinctions are actually disappearing. The essential structure of England is still almost what it was in the nineteenth century. But real differences between man and man are obviously diminishing, and this fact is grasped and even welcomed by people who only a few years ago were clinging desperately to their social prestige.

Whatever may be the ultimate fate of the very rich, the tendency of the working class and the middle class is evidently to merge. It may happen quickly or slowly, according to circumstances. It was accelerated by the war, and another ten years of all-round rationing, utility clothes, high income tax and compulsory national service may finish the process once and for all. The final effects of this we cannot foresee. There are observers, both native and foreign, who believe that the fairly large amount of individual freedom that is enjoyed in England depends on having a well-defined class system. Liberty, according to some, is incompatible with equality. But at least it is certain that the present drift *is* towards greater social equality, and that that is what the great mass of the English people desire.

1947.

Politics and the English Language

Most people who bother with the matter at all would admit that the English language is in a bad way, but it is generally assumed that we cannot by conscious action do anything about it. Our civilization is decadent and our language—so the argument runs—must inevitably share in the general collapse. It follows that any struggle against the abuse of language is a sentimental archaism, like preferring candles to electric light or hansom cabs to aeroplanes. Underneath this lies the half-conscious belief that language is a natural growth and not an instrument which we shape for our own purposes.

Now, it is clear that the decline of a language must ultimately have political and economic causes: it is not due simply to the bad influence of this or that individual writer. But an effect can become a cause, reinforcing the original cause and producing the same effect in an intensified form, and so on indefinitely. A man may take to drink because he feels himself to be a failure, and then fail all the more completely because he drinks. It is rather the same thing that is happening to the English language. It becomes ugly and inaccurate because our thoughts are foolish, but the slovenliness of our language makes it easier for us to have foolish thoughts. The point is that the process is reversible. Modern English, especially written English, is full of bad habits which spread by imitation and which can be avoided if one is willing to take the necessary trouble. If one gets rid of these habits one can think more clearly, and to think clearly is a necessary first step towards political regeneration: so that the fight against bad English is not frivolous and is not the exclusive concern of professional writers. I will come back to this presently, and I hope that by that time the meaning of what I have said here will have become clearer. Meanwhile, here are five specimens of the English language as it is now habitually written.

These five passages have not been picked out because they are especially bad—I could have quoted far worse if I had chosen—but because they illustrate various of the mental vices from which we now suffer. They are a little below the average, but are fairly representative samples. I number them so that I can refer back to them when necessary:

(1) "I am not, indeed, sure whether it is not true to say that the Milton who once seemed not unlike a seventeenth-century Shelley had not become, out of an experience ever more bitter in each year, more alien [*sic*] to the founder of that Jesuit sect which nothing could induce him to tolerate."
                    Professor Harold Laski (Essay in *Freedom of Expression*).

(2) "Above all, we cannot play ducks and drakes with a native battery of idioms which prescribes such egregious collocations of vocables as the Basic *put up with* for *tolerate* or *put at a loss* for *bewilder*."
                    Professor Lancelot Hogben (*Interglossa*).

(3) "On the one side we have the free personality: by definition it is not neurotic, for it has neither conflict nor dream. Its desires, such as they are, are transparent, for they are just what institutional approval keeps in the forefront of consciousness; another institutional pattern would alter their number and intensity; there is little in them that is natural, irreducible, or culturally dangerous. But *on the other side*, the social bond itself is nothing but the mutual reflection of these self-secure integrities. Recall the definition of love. Is not this the very picture of a small academic? Where is there a place in this hall of mirrors for either personality or fraternity?"
                    Essay on psychology in *Politics* (New York).

(4) "All the 'best people' from the gentlemen's clubs, and all the frantic fascist captains, united in common hatred of Socialism and bestial horror of the rising tide of the mass revolutionary movement, have turned to acts of provocation, to foul incendiarism, to medieval legends of poisoned wells, to legalize their own destruction of proletarian organizations, and rouse the agitated petty-bourgeoisie to chauvinistic fervour on behalf of the fight against the revolutionary way out of the crisis.'
                    Communist pamphlet

(5) "If a new spirit *is* to be infused into this old country, there is one thorny and contentious reform which must be tackled, and that is the humanization and galvanization of the B.B.C. Timidity here will bespeak canker and atrophy of the soul. The heart of Britain may be sound and of strong beat, for instance, but the British lion's roar at present is like that of Bottom in Shakespeare's *Midsummer Night's Dream*—as gentle as any sucking dove. A virile new Britain cannot continue indefinitely to be traduced in the eyes or rather ears, of the world by the effete languors of Langham Place, brazenly masquerading as 'standard English'. When the Voice of Britain is heard at nine o'clock, better far and infinitely less ludicrous to hear aitches honestly dropped than the present priggish, inflated, inhibited, school-ma'amish arch braying of blameless bashful mewing maidens!"

Letter in Tribune.

Each of these passages has faults of its own, but, quite apart from avoidable ugliness, two qualities are common to all of them. The first is staleness of imagery: the other is lack of precision. The writer either has a meaning and cannot express it, or he inadvertently says something else, or he is almost indifferent as to whether his words mean anything or not. This mixture of vagueness and sheer incompetence is the most marked characteristic of modern English prose, and especially of any kind of political writing. As soon as certain topics are raised, the concrete melts into the abstract and no one seems able to think of turns of speech that are not hackneyed: prose consists less and less of *words* chosen for the sake of their meaning, and more and more of *phrases* tacked together like the sections of a prefabricated hen-house. I list below, with notes and examples, various of the tricks by means of which the work of prose-construction is habitually dodged:

Dying Metaphors. A newly invented metaphor assists thought by evoking a visual image, while on the other hand a metaphor which is technically "dead" (e.g. *iron resolution*) has in effect reverted to being an ordinary word and can generally be used without loss of vividness. But in between these two classes there is a huge dump of worn-out metaphors which have lost all

evocative power and are merely used because they save people
the trouble of inventing phrases for themselves. Examples are
*Ring the changes on, take up the cudgels for, toe the line, ride rough-
shod over, stand shoulder to shoulder with, play into the hands of, no
axe to grind, grist to the mill, fishing in troubled waters, on the order
of the day, Achilles' heel, swan song, hotbed.* Many of these are
used without knowledge of their meaning (what is a "rift", for
instance?), and incompatible metaphors are frequently mixed, a
sure sign that the writer is not interested in what he is saying.
Some metaphors now current have been twisted out of their
original meaning without those who use them even being aware
of the fact. For example, *toe the line* is sometimes written *tow the
line.* Another example is *the hammer and the anvil,* now always
used with the implication that the anvil gets the worst of it. In
real life it is always the anvil that breaks the hammer, never the
other way about: a writer who stopped to think what he was
saying would be aware of this, and would avoid perverting the
original phrase.

Operators or *verbal false limbs.* These save the trouble of
picking out appropriate verbs and nouns, and at the same time
pad each sentence with extra syllables which give it an appearance
of symmetry. Characteristic phrases are: *render inoperative,
militate against, make contact with, be subjected to, give rise to, give
grounds for, have the effect of, play a leading part (role) in, make
itself felt, take effect, exhibit a tendency to, serve the purpose of, etc.
etc.* The keynote is the elimination of simple verbs. Instead of
being a single word, such as *break, stop, spoil, mend, kill,* a verb
becomes a *phrase,* made up of a noun or adjective tacked on to
some general-purposes verb such as *prove, serve, form, play,
render.* In addition, the passive voice is wherever possible used
in preference to the active, and noun constructions are used
instead of gerunds (*by examination of* instead of *by examining.*
The range of verbs is further cut down by means of the *-ize* and
de- formations, and the banal statements are given an appearance

of profundity by means of the *not un-* formation. Simple con-junctions and prepositions are replaced by such phrases as *with respect to, having regard to, the fact that, by dint of, in view of, in the interests of, on the hypothesis that*; and the ends of sentences are saved from anticlimax by such resounding commonplaces as *greatly to be desired, cannot be left out of account, a development to be expected in the near future, deserving of serious consideration, brought to a satisfactory conclusion*, and so on and so forth.

Pretentious diction. Words like *phenomenon, element, individual* (as noun), *objective, categorical, effective, virtual, basic, primary, promote, constitute, exhibit, exploit, utilize, eliminate, liquidate*, are used to dress up simple statement and give an air of scientific impartiality to biased judgments. Adjectives like *epoch-making, epic, historic, unforgettable, triumphant, age-old, inevitable, inexorable, veritable*, are used to dignify the sordid processes of international politics, while writing that aims at glorifying war usually takes on an archaic colour, its characteristic words being: *realm, throne, chariot, mailed fist, trident, sword, shield, buckler, banner, jackboot, clarion*. Foreign words and expressions such as *cul de sac, ancien régime, deus ex machina, mutatis mutandis, status quo, gleichschaltung, weltanschauung*, are used to give an air of culture and elegance. Except for the useful abbreviations *i.e., e.g.*, and *etc.*, there is no real need for any of the hundreds of foreign phrases now current in English. Bad writers, and especially scientific, political and sociological writers, are nearly always haunted by the notion that Latin or Greek words are grander than Saxon ones, and unnecessary words like *expedite, ameliorate, predict, extraneous, deracinated, clandestine, subaqueous* and hundreds of others constantly gain ground from their Anglo-Saxon opposite numbers.[1] The jargon peculiar to Marxist writing

[1] An interesting illustration of this is the way in which the English flower names which were in use till very recently are being ousted by Greek ones, *snapdragon* becoming *antirrhinum, forget-me-not* becoming *myosotis*, etc. It is hard to see any practical reason for this change of fashion: it is probably due to an instinctive turning-away from the more homely word and a vague feeling that the Greek word is scientific.

(*hyena, hangman, cannibal, petty bourgeois, these gentry, lacquey, flunkey, mad dog, White Guard,* etc.) consists largely of words and phrases translated from Russian, German or French; but the normal way of coining a new word is to use a Latin or Greek root with the appropriate affix and, where necessary, the -ize formation. It is often easier to make up words of this kind (*deregionalize, impermissible, extramarital, non-fragmentatory* and so forth) than to think up the English words that will cover one's meaning. The result, in general, is an increase in slovenliness and vagueness.

Meaningless words. In certain kinds of writing, particularly in art criticism and literary criticism, it is normal to come across long passages which are almost completely lacking in meaning.[1] Words like *romantic, plastic, values, human, dead, sentimental, natural, vitality,* as used in art criticism, are strictly meaningless, in the sense that they not only do not point to any discoverable object, but are hardly ever expected to do so by the reader. When one critic writes, "The outstanding feature of Mr. X's work is its living quality", while another writes, "The immediately striking thing about Mr. X's work is its peculiar deadness", the reader accepts this as a simple difference of opinion. If words like *black* and *white* were involved, instead of the jargon words *dead* and *living,* he would see at once that language was being used in an improper way. Many political words are similarly abused. The word *Fascism* has now no meaning except in so far as it signifies "something not desirable". The words *democracy, socialism, freedom, patriotic, realistic, justice,* have each of them several different meanings which cannot be reconciled with one another. In the case of a word like *democracy,* not only is there no

---

[1] Example: "Comfort's catholicity of perception and image, strangely Whitmanesque in range, almost the exact opposite in aesthetic compulsion, continues to evoke that trembling atmospheric accumulative hinting at a cruel, an inexorably serene timelessness . . . Wrey Gardiner scores by aiming at simple bull's-eyes with precision. Only they are not so simple, and through this contented sadness runs more than the surface bitter-sweet of resignation." (*Poetry Quarterly.*)

agreed definition, but the attempt to make one is resisted from all sides. It is almost universally felt that when we call a country democratic we are praising it: consequently the defenders of every kind of régime claim that it is a democracy, and fear that they might have to stop using the word if it were tied down to any one meaning. Words of this kind are often used in a consciously dishonest way. That is, the person who uses them has his own private definition, but allows his hearer to think he means something quite different. Statements like *Marshal Petain was a true patriot*, *The Soviet Press is the freest in the world*, *The Catholic Church is opposed to persecution*, are almost always made with intent to deceive. Other words used in variable meanings, in most cases more or less dishonestly, are: *class*, *totalitarian*, *science*, *progressive*, *reactionary*, *bourgeois*, *equality*.

Now that I have made this catalogue of swindles and perversions, let me give another example of the kind of writing that they lead to. This time it must of its nature be an imaginary one. I am going to translate a passage of good English into modern English of the worst sort. Here is a well-known verse from *Ecclesiastes*:

"I returned and saw under the sun, that the race is not to the swift, nor the battle to the strong, neither yet bread to the wise, nor yet riches to men of understanding, nor yet favour to men of skill; but time and chance happeneth to them all."

Here it is in modern English:

"Objective consideration of contemporary phenomena compels the conclusion that success or failure in competitive activities exhibits no tendency to be commensurate with innate capacity, but that a considerable element of the unpredictable must invariably be taken into account."

This is a parody, but not a very gross one. Exhibit (3), above, for instance, contains several patches of the same kind of English. It will be seen that I have not made a full translation. The beginning and ending of the sentence follow the original meaning fairly closely, but in the middle the concrete illustrations—race, battle, bread—dissolve into the vague phrase "success or failure in competitive activities". This had to be so, because no modern writer of the kind I am discussing—no one capable of using phrases like "objective consideration of contemporary phenomena"—would ever tabulate his thoughts in that precise and detailed way. The whole tendency of modern prose is away from concreteness. Now analyse these two sentences a little more closely. The first contains forty-nine words but only sixty syllables, and all its words are those of everyday life. The second contains thirty-eight words of ninety syllables: eighteen of its words are from Latin roots, and one from Greek. The first sentence contains six vivid images, and only one phrase ("time and chance") that could be called vague. The second contains not a single fresh, arresting phrase, and in spite of its ninety syllables it gives only a shortened version of the meaning contained in the first. Yet without a doubt it is the second kind of sentence that is gaining ground in modern English. I do not want to exaggerate. This kind of writing is not yet universal, and outcrops of simplicity will occur here and there in the worst-written page. Still, if you or I were told to write a few lines on the uncertainty of human fortunes, we should probably come much nearer to my imaginary sentence than to the one from *Ecclesiastes*.

As I have tried to show, modern writing at its worst does not consist in picking out words for the sake of their meaning and inventing images in order to make the meaning clearer. It consists in gumming together long strips of words which have already been set in order by someone else, and making the results presentable by sheer humbug. The attraction of this way of writing is that it is easy. It is easier—even quicker, once you have the habit—to say *In my opinion it is a not unjustifiable assumption that* than to say *I think*. If you use ready-made phrases, you not only don't have to hunt about for words; you also don't have to bother with the rhythms of your sentences, since these phrases are generally so arranged as to be more or less euphonious. When you are composing in a hurry—when you are dictating to a stenographer, for instance, or making a public speech—it is natural to fall into a pretentious, Latinized style. Tags like *a consideration which we should do well to bear in mind* or *a conclusion to which all of us would readily assent* will save many a sentence from coming down with a bump. By using stale metaphors, similes and idioms, you save much mental effort, at the cost of leaving your meaning vague, not only for your reader but for yourself. This is the significance of mixed metaphors. The sole aim of a metaphor is to call up a visual image. When these images clash—as in *The Fascist octupus has sung its swan song, the jackboot is thrown into the melting pot*—it can be taken as certain that the writer is not seeing a mental image of the objects he is naming; in other words he is not really thinking. Look again at the examples I gave at the beginning of this essay. Professor Laski (1) uses five negatives in fifty-three words. One of these is superfluous, making nonsense of the whole passage, and in addition there is the slip *alien* for akin, making further nonsense, and several avoidable pieces of clumsiness which increase the general vagueness. Professor Hogben (2) plays ducks and drakes with a battery which is able to write prescriptions, and, while disapproving of the everyday phrase *put up with*, is unwilling to look *egregious* up in the dictionary and see what it means. (3), if one takes an uncharitable attitude towards it, is simply meaningless: probably one could work out its intended meaning by reading the whole of the article in which it occurs. In (4), the writer knows more or less what he wants to say, but an accumulation of stale phrases chokes him like tea leaves blocking a sink. In (5), words and meaning have almost parted company. People who write in this manner usually have a general emotional meaning—they dislike one thing and want to express solidarity with another—but they are not interested in the detail of what they are saying. A scrupulous writer, in every sentence that he writes, will ask himself at least four questions, thus: What am I trying to say? What words will express it? What image or idiom will make it clearer? Is this image fresh enough to have an effect? And he will probably ask himself two more: Could I put it more shortly? Have I said anything that is avoidably ugly? But you are not obliged to go to all this trouble. You can shirk it by simply throwing your mind open and letting the ready-made phrases come crowding in. They will construct your sentences for you—even think your thoughts for you, to a certain extent—and at need they will perform the important service of partially concealing your meaning even from yourself. It is at this point that the special connexion between politics and the debasement of language becomes clear.

In our time it is broadly true that political writing is bad writing. Where it is not true, it will generally be found that the writer is some kind of rebel, expressing his private opinions and not a "party line". Orthodoxy, of whatever colour, seems to demand a lifeless, imitative style. The political dialects to be found in pamphlets, leading articles, manifestos, White Papers and the speeches of under-secretaries do, of course, vary from party to party, but they are all alike in that one almost never finds in them a fresh, vivid, home-made turn of speech. When one watches some tired hack on the platform mechanically repeating the familiar phrases—*bestial atrocities, iron heel, blood-stained tyranny, free peoples of the world, stand shoulder to shoulder* —one often has a curious feeling that one is not watching a live human being but some kind of dummy: a feeling which suddenly becomes stronger at moments when the light catches the speaker's spectacles and turns them into blank discs which seem to have no eyes behind them. And this is not altogether fanciful. A speaker who uses that kind of phraseology has gone some distance towards turning himself into a machine. The appropriate noises are coming out of his larynx, but his brain is not involved as it would be if he were choosing his words for himself. If the speech he is making is one that he is accustomed to make over and over again, he may be almost unconscious of what he is saying, as one is when one utters the responses in church. And this reduced state of consciousness, if not indispensable, is at any rate favourable to political conformity.

In our time, political speech and writings are largely the defence of the indefensible. Things like the continuance of British rule in India, the Russian purges and deportations, the dropping of the atom bombs on Japan, can indeed be defended, but only by arguments which are too brutal for most people to face, and which do not square with the professed aims of political parties. Thus political language has to consist largely of euphemism, question-begging and sheer cloudy vagueness. Defenceless villages are bombarded from the air, the inhabitants driven out into the countryside, the cattle machine-gunned, the huts set on fire with incendiary bullets: this is called *pacification*. Millions of peasants are robbed of their farms and sent trudging along the roads with no more than they can carry: this is called *transfer of population* or *rectification of frontiers*. People are imprisoned for years without trial, or shot in the back of the neck or sent to die of scurvy in Arctic lumber camps: this is called *elimination of unreliable elements*. Such phraseology is needed if one wants to name things without calling up mental pictures of them. Consider for instance some comfortable English professor defending Russian totalitarianism. He cannot say outright, "I believe in killing off your opponents when you can get good results by doing so." Probably, therefore, he will say something like this:

"While freely conceding that the Soviet régime exhibits certain features which the humanitarian may be inclined to deplore, we must, I think, agree that a certain curtailment of the right to political opposition is an unavoidable concomitant of transitional periods, and that the rigours which the Russian people have been called upon to undergo have been amply justified in the sphere of concrete achievement."

The inflated style is itself a kind of euphemism. A mass of

Latin words falls upon the facts like soft snow, blurring the outlines and covering up all the details. The great enemy of clear language is insincerity. When there is a gap between one's real and one's declared aims, one turns as it were instinctively to long words and exhausted idioms, like a cuttlefish squirting out ink. In our age there is no such thing as "keeping out of politics". All issues are political issues, and politics itself is a mass of lies, evasions, folly, hatred and schizophrenia. When the general atmosphere is bad, language must suffer. I should expect to find —this is a guess which I have not sufficient knowledge to verify— that the German, Russian and Italian languages have all deteriorated in the last ten or fifteen years, as a result of dictatorship.

But if thought corrupts language, language can also corrupt thought. A bad usage can spread by tradition and imitation, even among people who should and do know better. The debased language that I have been discussing is in some ways very convenient. Phrases like *a not unjustifiable assumption, leaves much to be desired, would serve no good purpose, a consideration which we should do well to bear in mind*, are a continuous temptation, a packet of aspirins always at one's elbow. Look back through this essay, and for certain you will find that I have again and again committed the very faults I am protesting against. By this morning's post I have received a pamphlet dealing with conditions in Germany. The author tells me that he "felt impelled" to write it. I open it at random, and here is almost the first sentence that I see: "(The Allies) have an opportunity not only of achieving a radical transformation of Germany's social and political structure in such a way as to avoid a nationalistic reaction in Germany itself, but at the same time of laying the foundations of a co-operative and unified Europe." You see, he "feels impelled" to write—feels, presumably, that he has something new to say—and yet his words, like cavalry horses answering the bugle, group themselves automatically into the familiar dreary pattern. This invasion of one's mind by ready-made phrases (*lay the foundations, achieve a radical transformation*) can only be prevented if one is constantly on guard against them, and every such phrase anaesthetizes a portion of one's brain.

I said earlier that the decadence of our language is probably curable. Those who deny this would argue, if they produced an argument at all, that language merely reflects existing social conditions, and that we cannot influence its development by any direct tinkering with words and constructions. So far as the general tone or spirit of a language goes, this may be true, but it is not true in detail. Silly words and expressions have often disappeared, not through any evolutionary process but owing to the conscious action of a minority. Two recent examples were *explore every avenue* and *leave no stone unturned*, which were killed by the jeers of a few journalists. There is a long list of flyblown metaphors which could similarly be got rid of if enough people would interest themselves in the job; and it should also be possible to laugh the *not un-* formation out of existence,[1] to reduce the amount of Latin and Greek in the average sentence, to drive out foreign phrases and strayed scientific words, and, in general, to make pretentiousness unfashionable. But all these are minor points. The defence of the English language implies more than this, and perhaps it is best to start by saying what it does *not* imply.

To begin with it has nothing to do with archaism, with the salvaging of obsolete words and turns of speech, or with the setting up of a "standard English" which must never be departed from. On the contrary, it is especially concerned with the scrapping of every word or idiom which has outworn its usefulness. It has nothing to do with correct grammar and syntax, which are of no importance so long as one makes one's meaning clear, or with the avoidance of Americanisms, or with having what is called a "good prose style". On the other hand it is not concerned

---

[1] One can cure oneself of the *not un-* formation by memorizing this sentence: *A not unblack dog was chasing a not unsmall rabbit across a not ungreen field.*

with fake simplicity and the attempt to make written English colloquial. Nor does it even imply in every case preferring the Saxon word to the Latin one, though it does imply using the fewest and shortest words that will cover one's meaning. What is above all needed is to let the meaning choose the word, and not the other way about. In prose, the worst thing one can do with words is to surrender to them. When you think of a concrete object, you think wordlessly, and then, if you want to describe the thing you have been visualizing you probably hunt about till you find the exact words that seem to fit it. When you think of something abstract you are more inclined to use words from the start, and unless you make a conscious effort to prevent it, the existing dialect will come rushing in and do the job for you, at the expense of blurring or even changing your meaning. Probably it is better to put off using words as long as possible and get one's meaning as clear as one can through pictures or sensations. Afterwards one can choose—not simply *accept*—the phrases that will best cover the meaning, and then switch round and decide what impression one's words are likely to make on another person. This last effort of the mind cuts out all stale or mixed images, all prefabricated phrases, needless repetitions, and humbug and vagueness generally. But one can often be in doubt about the effect of a word or a phrase, and one needs rules that one can rely on when instinct fails. I think the following rules will cover most cases:

(i) Never use a metaphor, simile or other figure of speech which you are used to seeing in print.

(ii) Never use a long word where a short one will do.

(iii) If it is possible to cut a word out, always cut it out.

(iv) Never use the passive where you can use the active.

(v) Never use a foreign phrase, a scientific word or a jargon word if you can think of an everyday English equivalent.

(vi) Break any of these rules sooner than say anything outright barbarous.

These rules sound elementary, and so they are, but they demand a deep change of attitude in anyone who has grown used to writing in the style now fashionable. One could keep all of them and still write bad English, but one could not write the kind of stuff that I quoted in those five specimens at the beginning of this article.

I have not here been considering the literary use of language, but merely language as an instrument for expressing and not for concealing or preventing thought. Stuart Chase and others have come near to claiming that all abstract words are meaningless, and have used this as a pretext for advocating a kind of political quietism. Since you don't know what Fascism is, how can you struggle against Fascism? One need not swallow such absurdities as this, but one ought to recognize that the present political chaos is connected with the decay of language, and that one can probably bring about some improvement by starting at the verbal end. If you simplify your English, you are freed from the worst follies of orthodoxy. You cannot speak any of the necessary dialects, and when you make a stupid remark its stupidity will be obvious, even to yourself. Political language—and with variations this is true of all political parties, from Conservatives to Anarchists—is designed to make lies sound truthful and murder respectable, and to give an appearance of solidity to pure wind. One cannot change this all in a moment, but one can at least change one's own habits, and from time to time one can even, if one jeers loudly enough, send some worn-out and useless phrase—some *jackboot, Achilles' heel, hotbed, melting pot, acid test, veritable inferno* or other lump of verbal refuse—into the dustbin where it belongs.

1946.

Writers and Leviathan

THE position of the writer in an age of State control is a subject that has already been fairly largely discussed, although most of the evidence that might be relevant is not yet available. In this place I do not want to express an opinion either for or against state patronage of the arts, but merely to point out that *what kind* of state rules over us must depend partly on the prevailing intellectual atmosphere: meaning, in this context, partly on the attitude of writers and artists themselves, and on their willingness or otherwise to keep the spirit of liberalism alive. If we find ourselves in ten years' time cringing before somebody like Zhdanov, it will probably be because that is what we have deserved. Obviously there are strong tendencies towards totalitarianism at work within the English literary intelligentsia already. But here I am not concerned with any organized and conscious movement such as Communism, but merely with the effect, on people of goodwill, of political thinking and the need to take sides politically.

This is a political age. War, Fascism, concentration camps, rubber truncheons, atomic bombs, etc., are what we daily think about, and therefore to a great extent what we write about, even when we do not name them openly. We cannot help this. When you are on a sinking ship, your thoughts will be about sinking ships. But not only is our subject matter narrowed, but our whole attitude towards literature is coloured by loyalties which we at least intermittently realize to be non-literary. I often have the feeling that even at the best of times literary criticism is fraudulent, since in the absence of any accepted standards whatever—any *external* reference which can give meaning to the statement that such and such a book is "good" or "bad"—every literary judgement consists in trumping up a set of rules to justify an instinctive preference. One's real reaction to a book, when one has a reaction at all, is usually "I like this book" or "I don't like it", and what follows is a rationalization. But "I like this book" is not, I think, a non-literary reaction: the non-literary reaction is: "This book is on my side, and therefore I must discover merits in it." Of course, when one praises a book for political reasons one may be emotionally sincere, in the sense that one does feel strong approval of it, but also it often happens that party solidarity demands a plain lie. Anyone used to reviewing books for political periodicals is well aware of this. In general, if you are writing for a paper that you are in agreement with, you sin by commission, and if for a paper of the opposite stamp, by omission. At any rate, innumerable controversial books—books for or against Soviet Russia, for or against Zionism, for or against the Catholic Church, etc.—are judged before they are read, and in effect before they are written. One knows in advance what reception they will get in what papers. And yet, with a dishonesty that sometimes is not even quarter-conscious, the pretence is kept up that genuinely literary standards are being applied.

Of course, the invasion of literature by politics was bound to happen. It must have happened, even if the special problem of totalitarianism had never arisen, because we have developed a sort of compunction which our grandparents did not have, an awareness of the enormous injustice and misery of the world, and a guilt-stricken feeling that one ought to be doing something about it, which makes a purely æsthetic attitude towards life impossible. No one, now, could devote himself to literature as single-mindedly as Joyce or Henry James. But unfortunately, to accept political responsibility now means yielding oneself over to orthodoxies and "party lines", with all the timidity and dishonesty that that implies. As against the Victorian writers, we have the disadvantage of living among clear-cut political ideologies and of usually knowing at a glance what thoughts are heretical. A modern literary intellectual lives and writes in constant dread—not, indeed, of public opinion in the wider sense, but of public opinion within his own group. As a rule, luckily, there is more than one group, but also at any given moment there is a dominant orthodoxy, to offend against which needs a thick skin and sometimes means cutting one's income in half for years on end. Obviously, for about fifteen years past, the dominant orthodoxy, especially among the young, has been "left". The key words are "progressive", "democratic" and "revolutionary", while the labels which you must at all costs avoid having gummed upon you are "bourgeois", "reactionary" and "Fascist". Almost everyone nowadays, even the majority of Catholics and Conservatives, is "progressive", or at least wishes to be thought so. No one, so far as I know, ever describes himself as a "bourgeois", just as no one literate enough to have heard the word ever admits to being guilty of anti-Semitism. We are all of us good democrats, anti-Fascist, anti-imperialist, contemptuous of class distinctions, impervious to colour prejudice, and so on and so forth. Nor is there much doubt that the present-day "left" orthodoxy is better than the rather snobbish, pietistic Conservative orthodoxy which prevailed twenty years ago, when the *Criterion* and (on a lower level) the *London Mercury* were the dominant literary magazines. For at the least its implied objective is a viable form of society which large numbers of people actually want. But it also has its own falsities which, because they cannot be admitted, make it impossible for certain questions to be seriously discussed.

The whole left-wing ideology, scientific and Utopian, was evolved by people who had no immediate prospect of attaining power. It was, therefore, an extremist ideology, utterly contemptuous of kings, governments, laws, prisons, police forces, armies, flags, frontiers, patriotism, religion, conventional morality, and, in fact, the whole existing scheme of things. Until well within living memory the forces of the left in all countries were fighting against a tyranny which appeared to be invincible, and it was easy to assume that if only *that* particular tyranny—

italism—could be overthrown, socialism would follow. More-
er, the left had inherited from liberalism certain distinctly
estionable beliefs, such as the belief that the truth will prevail
d persecution defeat itself, or that man is naturally good and
only corrupted by his environment. This perfectionist ideology
s persisted in nearly all of us, and it is in the name of it that we
test when (for instance) a Labour government votes huge
omes to the King's daughters or shows hesitation about
tionalizing steel. But we have also accumulated in our minds
whole series of unadmitted contradictions, as a result of
ccessive bumps against reality.

The first big bump was the Russian Revolution. For somewhat
nplex reasons, nearly the whole of the English left has been
ven to accept the Russian régime as "socialist", while silently
ognizing that its spirit and practice are quite alien to anything
it is meant by "socialism" in this country. Hence there has
sen a sort of schizophrenic manner of thinking, in which
rds like "democracy" can bear two irreconcilable meanings,
d such things as concentration camps and mass deportations
 be right and wrong simultaneously. The next blow to the
t-wing ideology was the rise of Fascism, which shook the
cifism and internationalism of the left without bringing about
definite restatement of doctrine. The experience of German
cupation taught the European peoples something that the
onial peoples knew already, namely, that class antagonisms
 not all-important and that there is such a thing as national
erest. After Hitler it was difficult to maintain seriously that
e enemy is in your own country" and that national independ-
ce is of no value. But though we all know this and act upon it
en necessary, we still feel that to say it aloud would be a kind
 treachery. And finally, the greatest difficulty of all, there
the fact that the left is now in power and is obliged to take
ponsibility and make genuine decisions.

Left governments almost invariably disappoint their sup-
rters because, even when the prosperity which they have

promised is achievable, there is always need of an uncomforta
transition period about which little has been said beforehand.
this moment we see our own government, in its desper
economic straits, fighting in effect against its own past pro
ganda. The crisis that we are now in is not a sudden unexpec
calamity, like an earthquake, and it was not caused by the w
but merely hastened by it. Decades ago it could be foreseen t
something of this kind was going to happen. Ever since
nineteenth century our national income, dependent partly
interest from foreign investments, and on assured markets a
cheap raw materials in colonial countries, had been extrem
precarious. It was certain that, sooner or later, someth
would go wrong and we should be forced to make our expo
balance our imports: and when that happened the Brit
standard of living, including the working-class standard,
bound to fall, at least temporarily. Yet the left-wing parties, e
when they were vociferously anti-imperialist, never made th
facts clear. On occasion they were ready to admit that
British workers had benefited, to some extent, by the looting
Asia and Africa, but they always allowed it to appear that
could give up our loot and yet in some way contrive to rem
prosperous. Quite largely, indeed, the workers were won over
socialism by being told that they were exploited, whereas
brute truth was that, in world terms, they were exploiters. N
to all appearances, the point has been reached when the worki
class living standard *cannot* be maintained, let alone raised. E
if we squeeze the rich out of existence, the mass of the peo
must either consume less or produce more. Or am I exaggerat
the mess we are in? I may be, and I should be glad to find my
mistaken. But the point I wish to make is that this questi
among people who are faithful to the left ideology, cannot
genuinely discussed. The lowering of wages and raising
working hours are felt to be inherently anti-socialist measur
and must therefore be dismissed in advance, whatever
economic situation may be. To suggest that they may

avoidable is merely to risk being plastered with those labels
t we are all terrified of. It is far safer to evade the issue and
tend that we can put everything right by redistributing the
sting national income.

To accept an orthodoxy is always to inherit unresolved
atradictions. Take for instance the fact that all sensitive
ple are revolted by industrialism and its products, and yet
aware that the conquest of poverty and the emancipation of
working class demand not less industrialization, but more
1 more. Or take the fact that certain jobs are absolutely
cessary and yet are never done except under some kind of
rcion. Or take the fact that it is impossible to have a positive
eign policy without having powerful armed forces. One could
ltiply examples. In every such case there is a conclusion
ich is perfectly plain but which can only be drawn if one is
vately disloyal to the official ideology. The normal response
o push the question, unanswered, into a corner of one's mind,
d then continue repeating contradictory catchwords. One does
t have to search far through the reviews and magazines to
cover the effects of this kind of thinking.

I am not, of course, suggesting that mental dishonesty is
culiar to socialists and left-wingers generally, or is commonest
ong them. It is merely that acceptance of *any* political
cipline seems to be incompatible with literary integrity. This
plies equally to movements like pacifism and personalism,
ich claim to be outside the ordinary political struggle. Indeed,
mere sound of words ending in -ism seems to bring with it
smell of propaganda. Group loyalties are necessary, and yet
y are poisonous to literature, so long as literature is the
oduct of individuals. As soon as they are allowed to have any
luence, even a negative one, on creative writing, the result
not only falsification, but often the actual drying-up of the
ventive faculties.

Well, then, what? Do we have to conclude that it is the duty
every writer to "keep out of politics"? Certainly not! In any

case, as I have said already, no thinking person can or d
genuinely keep out of politics, in an age like the present one
only suggest that we should draw a sharper distinction than
do at present between our political and our literary loyalties, a
should recognize that a willingness to *do* certain distasteful l
necessary things does not carry with it any obligation to swall
the beliefs that usually go with them. When a writer engages
politics he should do so as a citizen, as a human being, but
as a writer. I do not think that he has the right, merely on
score of his sensibilities, to shirk the ordinary dirty work
politics. Just as much as anyone else, he should be prepared
deliver lectures in draughty halls, to chalk pavements, to canv
voters, to distribute leaflets, even to fight in civil wars if it see
necessary. But whatever else he does in the service of his par
he should never write for it. He should make it clear that
writing is a thing apart. And he should be able to act
operatively while, if he chooses, completely rejecting the offic
ideology. He should never turn back from a train of thoug
because it may lead to a heresy, and he should not mind ve
much if his unorthodoxy is smelt out, as it probably will
Perhaps it is even a bad sign in a writer if he is not suspected
reactionary tendencies to-day, just as it was a bad sign if
was not suspected of Communist sympathies twenty ye
ago.

But does all this mean that a writer should not only refuse
be dictated to by political bosses, but also that he should refr
from writing *about* politics? Once again, certainly not! There
no reason why he should not write in the most crudely politi
way, if he wishes to. Only he should do so as an individual,
outsider, at the most an unwelcome guerrilla on the flank o
regular army. This attitude is quite compatible with ordina
political usefulness. It is reasonable, for example, to be willi
to fight in a war because one thinks the war ought to be wc
and at the same time to refuse to write war propagan
Sometimes, if a writer is honest, his writings and

political activities may actually contradict one another. There are occasions when that is plainly undesirable: but then the remedy is not to falsify one's impulses, but to remain silent.

To suggest that a creative writer, in a time of conflict, must split his life into two compartments, may seem defeatist or frivolous: yet in practice I do not see what else he can do. To lock yourself up in the ivory tower is impossible and undesirable. To yield subjectively, not merely to a party machine, but even to a group ideology, is to destroy yourself as a writer. We feel this dilemma to be a painful one, because we see the need of engaging in politics while also seeing what a dirty, degrading business it is. And most of us still have a lingering belief that every choice, even every political choice, is between good and evil, and that if a thing is necessary it is also right. We should, I think, get rid of this belief, which belongs to the nursery. In politics one can never do more than decide which of two evils is the less, and there are some situations from which one can only escape by acting like a devil or a lunatic. War, for example, may be necessary, but it is certainly not right or sane. Even a general election is not exactly a pleasant or edifying spectacle. If you have to take part in such things—and I think you do have to, unless you are armoured by old age or stupidity or hypocrisy —then you also have to keep part of yourself inviolate. For most people the problem does not arise in the same form, because their lives are split already. They are truly alive only in their leisure hours, and there is no emotional connexion between their work and their political activities. Nor are they generally asked, in the name of political loyalty, to debase themselves as workers. The artist, and especially the writer, is asked just that—in fact, it is the only thing that politicians ever ask of him. If he refuses, that does not mean that he is condemned to inactivity. One half of him, which in a sense is the whole of him, can act as resolutely, even as violently if need be, as anyone else. But his writings, in so far as they have any value, will always be the products of the saner self that stands aside, records the things that are done and admits their necessity, but refuses to be deceived as to their true nature.

1948.

Why I Write

From a very early age, perhaps the age of five or six, I knew that when I grew up I should be a writer. Between the ages of about seventeen and twenty-four I tried to abandon this idea, but I did so with the consciousness that I was outraging my true nature and that sooner or later I should have to settle down and write books.

I was the middle child of three, but there was a gap of five years on either side, and I barely saw my father before I was eight. For this and other reasons I was somewhat lonely, and I soon developed disagreeable mannerisms which made me unpopular throughout my schooldays. I had the lonely child's habit of making up stories and holding conversations with imaginary persons, and I think from the very start my literary ambitions were mixed up with the feeling of being isolated and undervalued. I knew that I had a facility with words and a power of facing unpleasant facts, and I felt that this created a sort of private world in which I could get my own back for my failure in everyday life. Nevertheless the volume of serious—i.e. seriously intended—writing which I produced all through my childhood and boyhood would not amount to half a dozen pages. I wrote my first poem at the age of four or five, my mother taking it down to dictation. I cannot remember anything about it except that it was about a tiger and the tiger had "chair-like teeth"—a good enough phrase, but I fancy the poem was a plagiarism of Blake's "Tiger, Tiger". At eleven, when the war of 1914–18 broke out, I wrote a patriotic poem which was printed in the local newspaper, as was another, two years later, on the death of Kitchener. From time to time, when I was a bit older, I wrote bad and usually unfinished "nature poems" in the Georgian style. I also, about twice, attempted a short story which was a ghastly failure. That was the total of the would-be serious work that I actually set down on paper during all those years.

However, throughout this time I did in a sense engage in literary activities. To begin with there was the made-to-order stuff which I produced quickly, easily and without much pleasure to myself. Apart from school work, I wrote *vers d'occasion*, semi-comic poems which I could turn out at what now seems to me astonishing speed—at fourteen I wrote a whole rhyming play, in imitation of Aristophanes, in about a week—and helped to edit school magazines, both printed and in manuscript. These magazines were the most pitiful burlesque stuff that you could imagine, and I took far less trouble with them than I now would with the cheapest journalism. But side by side with all this, for fifteen years or more, I was carrying out a literary exercise of a quite different kind: this was the making up of a continuous "story" about myself, a sort of diary existing only in the mind. I believe this is a common habit of children and adolescents. As a very small child I used to imagine that I was, say, Robin Hood, and picture myself as the hero of thrilling adventures, but quite soon my "story" ceased to be narcissistic in a crude way and became more and more a mere description of what I was doing and the things I saw. For minutes at a time this kind of thing would be running through my head: "He pushed the door open and entered the room. A yellow beam of sunlight, filtering through the muslin curtains, slanted on to the table, where a matchbox, half open, lay beside the inkpot. With his right hand in his pocket he moved across to the window. Down in the street a tortoiseshell cat was chasing a dead leaf," etc., etc. This habit continued till I was about twenty-five, right through my non-literary years. Although I had to search, and did search, for the right words, I seemed to be making this descriptive effort almost against my will, under a kind of compulsion from outside. The "story" must, I suppose, have reflected the styles of the various writers I admired at different ages, but so far as I remember it always had the same meticulous descriptive quality.

When I was about sixteen I suddenly discovered the joy of mere words, i.e. the sounds and associations of words. The lines from *Paradise Lost*—

> So hee with difficulty and labour hard
> Moved on: with difficulty and labour hee,

which do not now seem to me so very wonderful, sent shivers down my backbone; and the spelling "hee" for "he" was an added pleasure. As for the need to describe things, I knew all about it already. So it is clear what kind of books I wanted to write, in so far as I could be said to want to write books at that time. I wanted to write enormous naturalistic novels with unhappy endings, full of detailed descriptions and arresting similes, and also full of purple passages in which words were used partly for the sake of their sound. And in fact my first completed novel, *Burmese Days*, which I wrote when I was thirty but projected much earlier, is rather that kind of book.

I give all this background information because I do not think one can assess a writer's motives without knowing something of his early development. His subject matter will be determined by the age he lives in—at least this is true in tumultuous, revolutionary ages like our own—but before he ever begins to write he will have acquired an emotional attitude from which he will never completely escape. It is his job, no doubt, to discipline his temperament and avoid getting stuck at some immature stage, or in some perverse mood: but if he escapes from his early influences altogether, he will have killed his impulse to write. Putting aside the need to earn a living, I think there are four great motives for writing, at any rate for writing prose. They exist in different degrees in every writer, and in any one writer the proportions will vary from time to time, according to the atmosphere in which he is living. They are:

(1) Sheer egoism. Desire to seem clever, to be talked about, to be remembered after death, to get your own back on grown-ups who snubbed you in childhood, etc., etc. It is humbug to pretend

that this is not a motive, and a strong one. Writers share this characteristic with scientists, artists, politicians, lawyers, soldiers, successful businessmen—in short, with the whole top crust of humanity. The great mass of human beings are not acutely selfish. After the age of about thirty they abandon individual ambition—in many cases, indeed, they almost abandon the sense of being individuals at all—and live chiefly for others, or are simply smothered under drudgery. But there is also the minority of gifted, wilful people who are determined to live their own lives to the end, and writers belong in this class. Serious writers, I should say, are on the whole more vain and self-centred than journalists, though less interested in money.

(2) Æsthetic enthusiasm. Perception of beauty in the external world, or, on the other hand, in words and their right arrangement. Pleasure in the impact of one sound on another, in the firmness of good prose or the rhythm of a good story. Desire to share an experience which one feels is valuable and ought not to be missed. The æsthetic motive is very feeble in a lot of writers, but even a pamphleteer or a writer of textbooks will have pet words and phrases which appeal to him for non-utilitarian reasons; or he may feel strongly about typography, width of margins, etc. Above the level of a railway guide, no book is quite free from æsthetic considerations.

(3) Historical impulse. Desire to see things as they are, to find out true facts and store them up for the use of posterity.

(4) Political purpose—using the word "political" in the widest possible sense. Desire to push the world in a certain direction, to alter other people's idea of the kind of society that they should strive after. Once again, no book is genuinely free from political bias. The opinion that art should have nothing to do with politics is itself a political attitude.

It can be seen how these various impulses must war against one another, and how they must fluctuate from person to person and from time to time. By nature—taking your "nature" to be the state you have attained when you are first adult—I am a person in whom the first three motives would outweigh the fourth. In a peaceful age I might have written ornate or merely descriptive books, and might have remained almost unaware of my political loyalties. As it is I have been forced into becoming a sort of pamphleteer. First I spent five years in an unsuitable profession (the Indian Imperial Police, in Burma), and then I underwent poverty and the sense of failure. This increased my natural hatred of authority and made me for the first time fully aware of the existence of the working classes, and the job in Burma had given me some understanding of the nature of imperialism: but these experiences were not enough to give me an accurate political orientation. Then came Hitler, the Spanish civil war, etc. By the end of 1935 I had still failed to reach a firm decision.

The Spanish war and other events in 1936–7 turned the scale and thereafter I knew where I stood. Every line of serious work that I have written since 1936 has been written, directly or indirectly, *against* totalitarianism and *for* democratic socialism, as I understand it. It seems to me nonsense, in a period like our own, to think that one can avoid writing of such subjects. Everyone writes of them in one guise or another. It is simply a question of which side one takes and what approach one follows. And the more one is conscious of one's political bias, the more chance one has of acting politically without sacrificing one's æsthetic and intellectual integrity.

What I have most wanted to do throughout the past ten years is to make political writing into an art. My starting point is always a feeling of partisanship, a sense of injustice. When I sit down to write a book, I do not say to myself, "I am going to produce a work of art." I write it because there is some lie that I want to expose, some fact to which I want to draw attention, and my initial concern is to get a hearing. But I could not do the work of writing a book, or even a long magazine article, if it were not also an æsthetic experience. Anyone who cares to examine my work will see that even when it is downright propaganda it contains much that a full-time politician would consider irrelevant. I am not able, and I do not want, completely to abandon the world-view that I acquired in childhood. So long as I remain alive and well I shall continue to feel strongly about prose style, to love the surface of the earth, and to take a pleasure in solid objects and scraps of useless information. It is no use trying to suppress that side of myself. The job is to reconcile my ingrained likes and dislikes with the essentially public, non-individual activities that this age forces on all of us.

It is not easy. It raises problems of construction and of language, and it raises in a new way the problem of truthfulness. Let me give just one example of the cruder kind of difficulty that arises. My book about the Spanish civil war, *Homage to Catalonia,* is, of course, a frankly political book, but in the main it is written with a certain detachment and regard for form. I did try very hard in it to tell the whole truth without violating my literary instincts. But among other things it contains a long chapter, full of newspaper quotations and the like, defending the Trotskyists who were accused of plotting with Franco. Clearly such a chapter, which after a year or two would lose its interest for any ordinary reader, must ruin the book. A critic whom I respect read me a lecture about it. "Why did you put in all that stuff?" he said. "You've turned what might have been a good book into journalism." What he said was true, but I could not have done otherwise. I happened to know, what very few people in England had been allowed to know, that innocent men were being falsely accused. If I had not been angry about that I should never have written the book.

In one form or another this problem comes up again. The problem of language is subtler and would take too long to discuss. I will only say that of late years I have tried to write less picturesquely and more exactly. In any case I find that by the time you have perfected any style of writing, you have always outgrown it. *Animal Farm* was the first book in which I tried, with full consciousness of what I was doing, to fuse political purpose and artistic purpose into one whole. I have not written a novel for seven years, but I hope to write another fairly soon. It is bound to be a failure, every book is a failure, but I do know with some clarity what kind of book I want to write.

Looking back through the last page or two, I see that I have made it appear as though my motives in writing were wholly public-spirited. I don't want to leave that as the final impression. All writers are vain, selfish and lazy, and at the very bottom of their motives there lies a mystery. Writing a book is a horrible, exhausting struggle, like a long bout of some painful illness. One would never undertake such a thing if one were not driven on by some demon whom one can neither resist nor understand. For all one knows that demon is simply the same instinct that makes a baby squall for attention. And yet it is also true that one can write nothing readable unless one constantly struggles to efface one's own personality. Good prose is like a window pane. I cannot say with certainty which of my motives are the strongest, but I know which of them deserve to be followed. And looking back through my work, I see that it is invariably where I lacked a *political* purpose that I wrote lifeless books and was betrayed into purple passages, sentences without meaning, decorative adjectives and humbug generally.

1947.

Poetry and the Microphone

About a year ago I and a number of others were engaged in broadcasting programmes to India, and among other things we broadcast a good deal of verse by contemporary and near-contemporary English writers—for example, Eliot, Herbert Read, Auden, Spender, Dylan Thomas, Henry Treece, Alex Comfort, Robert Bridges, Edmund Blunden, D. H. Lawrence. Whenever it was possible we had poems broadcast by the people who wrote them. Just why these particular programmes (a small and remote outflanking movement in the radio war) were instituted there is no need to explain here, but I should add that the fact that we were broadcasting to an Indian audience dictated our technique to some extent. The essential point was that our literary broadcasts were aimed at the Indian university students, a small and hostile audience, unapproachable by anything that could be described as British propaganda. It was known in advance that we could not hope for more than a few thousand listeners at the most, and this gave us an excuse to be more "highbrow" than is generally possible on the air.

If you are broadcasting poetry to people who know your language but don't share your cultural background, a certain amount of comment and explanation is unavoidable, and the formula we usually followed was to broadcast what purported to be a monthly literary magazine. The editorial staff were supposedly sitting in their office, discussing what to put into the next number. Somebody suggested one poem, someone else suggested another. There was a short discussion and then came the poem itself, read in a different voice, preferably the author's own. This poem naturally called up another, and so the programme continued, usually with at least half a minute of discussion between any two items. For a half-hour programme, six voices seemed to be the best number. A programme of this sort was necessarily somewhat shapeless, but it could be given a certain appearance of unity by making it revolve round a single central theme. For example, one number of our imaginary magazine was devoted to the subject of war. It included two poems by Edmund Blunden, Auden's *September, 1941*, extracts from a long poem by G. S. Fraser (*A Letter to Anne Ridler*), Byron's *Isles of Greece* and an extract from T. E. Lawrence's *Revolt in the Desert*. These half-dozen items, with the arguments that preceded and followed them, covered reasonably well the possible attitudes towards war. The poems and the prose extract took about twenty minutes to broadcast, the arguments about eight minutes.

This formula may seem slightly ridiculous and also rather patronizing, but its advantage is that the element of mere instruction, the textbook motif, which is quite unavoidable if one is going to broadcast serious and sometimes "difficult" verse, becomes a lot less forbidding when it appears as an informal discussion. The various speakers can ostensibly say to one another what they are in reality saying to the audience. Also, by such an approach you at least give a poem a context, which is just what poetry lacks from the average man's point of view. But of course there are other methods. One which we frequently used was to set a poem in music. It is announced that in a few minutes' time such and such a poem will be broadcast; then the music plays for perhaps a minute, then fades out into the poem, which follows without any title or announcement, then the music is faded in again and plays up for another minute or two—the whole thing taking perhaps five minutes. It is necessary to choose appropriate music, but needless to say, the real purpose of the music is to insulate the poem from the rest of the programme. By this method you can have, say, a Shakespeare sonnet within three minutes of a news bulletin without, at any rate to my ear, any gross incongruity.

These programmes that I have been speaking of were of no great value in themselves, but I have mentioned them because of the ideas they aroused in myself and some others about the possibilities of the radio as a means of popularizing poetry. I was early struck by the fact that the broadcasting of a poem by the person who wrote it does not merely produce an effect upon the audience, if any, but also on the poet himself. One must remember that extremely little in the way of broadcasting poetry has been done in England, and that many people who write verse have never even considered the idea of reading it aloud. By being set down at a microphone, especially if this happens at all regularly, the poet is brought into a new relationship with his work, not otherwise attainable in our time and country. It is a commonplace that in modern times—the last two hundred years, say—poetry has come to have less and less connexion either with music or with the spoken word. It needs print in order to exist at all, and it is no more expected that a poet, as such, will know how to sing or even declaim than it is expected that an architect will know how to plaster a ceiling. Lyrical and rhetorical poetry have almost ceased to be written, and a hostility towards poetry on the part of the common man has come to be taken for granted in any country where everyone can read. And where such a breach exists it is always inclined to widen, because the concept of poetry as primarily something printed, and something intelligible only to a minority, encourages obscurity and "cleverness". How many people do not feel quasi-instinctively that there must be something wrong with any poem whose meaning can be taken in at a single glance? It seems unlikely that these tendencies will be checked unless it again becomes normal to read verse aloud, and it is difficult to see how this can be brought about except by using the radio as a medium. But the special advantage of the radio, its power to select the right audience, and to do away with stage-fright and embarrassment, ought here to be noticed.

In broadcasting your audience is conjectural, but it is an audience of *one*. Millions may be listening, but each is listening alone, or as a member of a small group, and each has (or ought have) the feeling that you are speaking to him individually. More than this it is reasonable to assume that your audience is sympathetic, or at least interested, for anyone who is bored can promptly switch you off by turning a knob. But though presumably sympathetic, the audience *has no power over you*. It just here that a broadcast differs from a speech or a lecture. On the platform, as anyone used to public speaking knows, it is almost impossible not to take your tone from the audience. It is always obvious within a few minutes what they will respond to and what they will not, and in practice you are almost compelled to speak for the benefit of what you estimate as the stupidest person present, and also to ingratiate yourself by means of the ballyhoo known as "personality". If you don't do so, the result always an atmosphere of frigid embarrassment. That grisly thing, a "poetry reading", is what it is because there will always be some among the audience who are bored or all but frankly hostile and who can't remove themselves by the simple act of turning a knob. And it is at bottom the same difficulty—the fact that a theatre audience is not a selected one—that makes it impossible to get a decent performance of Shakespeare in England. On the air these conditions do not exist. The poet *feels* that he is addressing people to whom poetry means something, and it is a fact that poets who are used to broadcasting can read into the microphone with a virtuosity they would not equal if they had a visible audience in front of them. The element of make-believe that enters here does not greatly matter. The point that in the only way now possible the poet has been brought into a situation in which reading verse aloud seems a natural unembarrassing thing, a normal exchange between man and man: also he has been led to think of this work as *sound* rather than as a pattern on paper. By that much the reconciliation between poetry and the common man is nearer. It already exists the poet's end of the ether-waves, whatever may be happening the other end.

However, what is happening at the other end cannot be

disregarded. It will be seen that I have been speaking as though the whole subject of poetry were embarrassing, almost indecent as though popularizing poetry were essentially a strategic manœuvre, like getting a dose of medicine down a child's throat or establishing tolerance for a persecuted sect. But unfortunately that or something like it is the case. There can be no doubt that in our civilization poetry is by far the most discredited of the arts, the only art, indeed, in which the average man refuses to discern *any* value. Arnold Bennett was hardly exaggerating when he said that in the English-speaking countries, the word "poetry" would disperse a crowd quicker than a fire hose. And as I have pointed out, a breach of this kind tends to widen simply because of its existence, the common man becoming more and more anti-poetry, the poet more and more arrogant and unintelligible, until the divorce between poetry and popular culture is accepted as a sort of law of Nature, although in fact it belongs only to our own time and to a comparatively small area of the earth. We live in an age in which the average human being in the highly civilized countries is æsthetically inferior to the lowest savage. This state of affairs is generally looked upon as being incurable by any *conscious* act, and on the other hand is expected to right itself of its own accord as soon as society takes a comelier shape. With slight variations the Marxist, the anarchist and the religious believer will all tell you this, and in broad terms it is undoubtedly true. The ugliness amid which we live has spiritual and economic causes and is not to be explained by the mere going-astray of tradition at some point or other. But it does not follow that no improvement is possible within our present framework, nor that an æsthetic improvement is not a necessary part of the general redemption of society. It is worth stopping to wonder, therefore, whether it would not be possible even now to rescue poetry from its special position as the most hated of the arts and win for it at least the same degree of toleration as exists for music. But one has to start by asking, in what way and to what extent is poetry unpopular?

On the face of it, the unpopularity of poetry is as complete as could be. But on second thoughts, this has to be qualified in a rather peculiar way. To begin with, there is still an appreciable amount of folk poetry (nursery rhymes, etc.) which is universally known and quoted and forms part of the background of everyone's mind. There is also a handful of ancient songs and ballads which have never gone out of favour. In addition there is also the popularity, or at least the toleration, of "good bad" poetry, generally of a patriotic or sentimental kind. This might seem beside the point if it were not that "good bad" poetry has all the characteristics which, ostensibly, make the average man dislike true poetry. It is in verse, it rhymes, it deals in lofty sentiments and unusual language—all this to a very marked degree, for it is almost axiomatic that bad poetry is more "poetical" than good poetry. Yet if not actively liked it is at least tolerated. For example, just before writing this I have been listening to a couple of B.B.C. comedians doing their usual turn before the nine o'clock news. In the last three minutes one of the two comedians suddenly announces that he "wants to be serious for a moment" and proceeds to recite a piece of patriotic balderdash entitled *A Fine Old English Gentleman*, in praise of His Majesty the King. Now, what is the reaction of the audience to this sudden lapse into the worst sort of rhyming heroics? It cannot be very violently negative, or there would be a sufficient volume of indignant letters to stop the B.B.C. doing this kind of thing. One must conclude that though the big public is hostile to *poetry*, it is not strongly hostile to *verse*. After all, if rhyme and metre were disliked for their own sakes, neither songs nor dirty limericks could be popular. Poetry is disliked because it is associated with unintelligibility, intellectual pretentiousness and a general feeling of Sunday-on-a-weekday. Its name creates in advance the same sort of bad impression as the word "God", or a parson's dog-collar. To a certain extent, popularizing poetry is a question of breaking down an acquired inhibition. It is a question of getting people to listen instead of uttering a

mechanical raspberry. If true poetry could be introduced to th
big public in such a way as to make it seem *normal*, as that piec
of rubbish I have just listened to presumably seemed norma
then part of the prejudice against it might be overcome.

It is difficult to believe that poetry can ever be popularize
again without some deliberate effort at the education of publi
taste, involving strategy and perhaps even subterfuge. T. S
Eliot once suggested that poetry, particularly dramatic poetry
might be brought back into the consciousness of ordinary peopl
through the medium of the music hall; he might have added th
pantomime, whose vast possibilities do not seem ever to hav
been completely explored. *Sweeney Agonistes* was perhap
written with some such idea in mind, and it would in fact b
conceivable as a music-hall turn, or at least as a scene in a revue
I have suggested the radio as a more hopeful medium, and
have pointed out its technical advantages, particularly from th
point of view of the poet. The reason why such a suggestio
sounds hopeless at first hearing is that few people are able t
imagine the radio being used for the dissemination of anythin
except tripe. People listen to the stuff that does actually dribbl
from the loudspeakers of the world, and conclude that it is fo
that and nothing else that the wireless exists. Indeed the ver
word "wireless" calls up a picture either of roaring dictators o
of genteel throaty voices announcing that three of our aircra
have failed to return. Poetry on the air sounds like the Muse
in striped trousers. Nevertheless one ought not to confuse th
capabilities of an instrument with the use it is actually put to
Broadcasting is what it is, not because there is something in
herently vulgar, silly and dishonest about the whole apparatu
of microphone and transmitter, but because all the broadcastin
that now happens all over the world is under the control o
governments or great monopoly companies which are activel
interested in maintaining the *status quo* and therefore in pre
venting the common man from becoming too intelligent
Something of the same kind has happened to the cinema

which, like the radio, made its appearance during the monopoly stage of capitalism and is fantastically expensive to operate. In all the arts the tendency is similar. More and more the channels of production are under the control of bureaucrats, whose aim is to destroy the artist or at least to castrate him. This would be a bleak outlook if it were not that the totalitarianization which is now going on, and must undoubtedly continue to go on, in every country of the world, is mitigated by another process which it was not easy to foresee even as short a time as five years ago.

This is, that the huge bureaucratic machines of which we are all part are beginning to work creakily because of their mere size and their constant growth. The tendency of the modern state is to wipe out the freedom of the intellect, and yet at the same time every state, especially under the pressure of war, finds itself more and more in need of an intelligentsia to do its publicity for it. The modern state needs, for example, pamphlet-writers, poster artists, illustrators, broadcasters, lecturers, film producers, actors, song-composers, even painters and sculptors, not to mention psychologists, sociologists, bio-chemists, mathematicians and what-not. The British government started the last war with the more or less openly declared intention of keeping the literary intelligentsia out of it; yet after three years of war almost every writer, however undesirable his political history or opinions, was sucked into the various Ministries or the B.B.C., and even those who entered the armed forces tended to find themselves after a while in Public Relations or some other essentially literary job. The Government absorbed these people, unwillingly enough, because it found itself unable to get on without them. The ideal, from the official point of view, would have been to put all publicity into the hands of "safe" people like A. P. Herbert or Ian Hay: but since not enough of these were available, the existing intelligentsia had to be utilized, and the tone and even to some extent the content of official propaganda have been modified accordingly. No one acquainted with the Government pamphlets, A.B.C.A. lectures, documentary films and broadcasts to occupied countries which have been issued during the war imagines that our rulers would sponsor this kind of thing if they could help it. Only, the bigger the machine of government becomes, the more loose ends and forgotten corners there are in it. This is perhaps a small consolation, but it is not a despicable one. It means that in countries where there is already a strong liberal tradition, bureaucratic tyranny can perhaps never be complete. The striped-trousered ones will rule, but so long as they are forced to maintain an intelligentsia, the intelligentsia will have a certain amount of autonomy. If the Government needs, for example, documentary films, it must employ people specially interested in the technique of the film, and it must allow them the necessary minimum of freedom; consequently, films that are all wrong from the bureaucratic point of view will always have a tendency to appear. So also with painting, photography, script-writing, reportage, lecturing and all the other arts and half-arts of which a complex modern state has need.

The application of this to the radio is obvious. At present the loudspeaker is the enemy of the creative writer, but this may not necessarily remain true when the volume and scope of broadcasting increase. As things are, although the radio does keep up a feeble show of interest in contemporary literature, it is harder to capture five minutes on the air in which to broadcast a poem than twelve hours in which to disseminate lying propaganda, tinned music, stale jokes, faked "discussions" or what-have-you. But that state of affairs may alter in the way I have indicated, and when that time comes serious experiment in the broadcasting of verse, with complete disregard for the various hostile influences which prevent any such thing at present, would become possible. I don't claim it as certain that such an experiment would have very great results. The radio was bureaucratized so early in its career that the relationship between broadcasting and literature has never been thought out. It is not certain that the microphone is the instrument by which poetry could be brought back to the common people and it is not even certain that poetry would gain by being more of a spoken and less of a written thing. But I do urge that these possibilities exist, and that those who care for literature might turn their minds more often to this much-despised medium, whose powers for good have perhaps been obscured by the voices of Professor Joad and Doctor Goebbels.

1945.

Boys' Weeklies

You never walk far through any poor quarter in any big town without coming upon a small newsagent's shop. The general appearance of these shops is always very much the same: a few posters for the *Daily Mail* and the *News of the World* outside, a poky little window with sweet-bottles and packets of Players, and a dark interior smelling of liquorice allsorts and festooned from floor to ceiling with vilely printed twopenny papers, most of them with lurid cover-illustrations in three colours.

Except for the daily and evening papers, the stock of these shops hardly overlaps at all with that of the big newsagents. Their main selling line is the twopenny weekly, and the number and variety of these are almost unbelievable. Every hobby and pastime—cage-birds, fretwork, carpentering, bees, carrier-pigeons, home conjuring, philately, chess—has at least one paper devoted to it, and generally several. Gardening and livestock-keeping must have at least a score between them. Then there are the sporting papers, the radio papers, the children's comics, the various snippet papers such as *Tit-bits*, the large range of papers devoted to the movies and all more or less exploiting women's legs, the various trade papers, the women's story-papers (the *Oracle*, *Secrets*, *Peg's Paper*, etc., etc.), the needlework papers—these so numerous that a display of them alone will often fill an entire window—and in addition the long series of "Yank Mags" (*Fight Stories*, *Action Stories*, *Western Short Stories*, etc.), which are imported shop-soiled from America and sold at twopence halfpenny or threepence. And the periodical proper shades off into the fourpenny novelette, the *Aldine Boxing Novels*, the *Boys' Friend Library*, the *Schoolgirls' Own Library* and many others.

Probably the contents of these shops is the best available indication of what the mass of the English people really feels and thinks. Certainly nothing half so revealing exists in documentary form. Best-seller novels, for instance, tell one a great deal, but the novel is aimed almost exclusively at people above the £4-a-week level. The movies are probably a very unsafe guide to popular taste, because the film industry is virtually a monopoly, which means that it is not obliged to study its public at all closely. The same applies to some extent to the daily papers, and most of all to the radio. But it does not apply to the weekly paper with a smallish circulation and specialized subject-matter. Papers like the *Exchange and Mart*, for instance, or *Cage-birds*, or the *Oracle*, or the *Prediction*, or the *Matrimonial Times*, only exist because there is a definite demand for them, and they reflect the minds of their readers as a great national daily with a circulation of millions cannot possibly do.

Here I am only dealing with a single series of papers, the boys' twopenny weeklies, often inaccurately described as "penny dreadfuls". Falling strictly within this class there are at present ten papers, the *Gem, Magnet, Modern Boy, Triumph* and *Champion*, all owned by the Amalgamated Press, and the *Wizard, Rover, Skipper, Hotspur* and *Adventure*, all owned by D. C. Thomson & Co. What the circulation of these papers are, I do not know. The editors and proprietors refuse to name any figures, and in any case the circulation of a paper carrying serial stories is bound to fluctuate widely. But there is no question that the combined public of the ten papers is a very large one. They are on sale in every town in England, and nearly every boy who reads at all goes through a phase of reading one or more of them. The *Gem* and *Magnet*, which are much the oldest of these papers, are of rather different type from the rest, and they have evidently lost some of their popularity during the past few years. A good many boys now regard them as old fashioned and "slow". Nevertheless I want to discuss them first, because they are more interesting psychologically than the others, and also because the mere survival of such papers into the nineteen-thirties is a rather startling phenomenom.

The *Gem* and *Magnet* are sister-papers (characters out of one paper frequently appear in the other), and were both started more than thirty years ago. At that time, together with *Chums* and the old *B.O.P.*, they were the leading papers for boys, and they remained dominant till quite recently. Each of them carries every week a fifteen- or twenty-thousand-word school story, complete in itself, but usually more or less connected with the story of the week before. The *Gem* in addition to its school story carries one or more adventure serial. Otherwise the two papers are so much alike that they can be treated as one, though the *Magnet* has always been the better known of the two, probably because it possesses a really first-rate character in the fat boy, Billy Bunter.

The stories are stories of what purports to be public-school life, and the schools (Greyfriars in the *Magnet* and St. Jim's in the *Gem*) are represented as ancient and fashionable foundations of the type of Eton or Winchester. All the leading characters are fourth-form boys aged fourteen or fifteen, older or younger boys only appearing in very minor parts. Like Sexton Blake and Nelson Lee, these boys continue week after week and year after year, never growing any older. Very occasionally a new boy arrives or a minor character drops out, but in at any rate the last twenty-five years the personnel has barely altered. All the principal characters in both papers—Bob Cherry, Tom Merry, Harry Wharton, Johnny Bull, Billy Bunter and the rest of them —were at Greyfriars or St. Jim's long before the Great War, exactly the same age as at present, having much the same kind of adventures and talking almost exactly the same dialect. And not only the characters but the whole atmosphere of both *Gem* and *Magnet* has been preserved unchanged, partly by means of very elaborate stylization. The stories in the *Magnet* are signed "Frank Richards" and those in the *Gem*, "Martin Clifford", but a series lasting thirty years could hardly be the work of the same

person every week.[1] Consequently they have to be written in a
style that is easily imitated—an extraordinary, artificial, repetitive
style, quite different from anything else now existing in English
literature. A couple of extracts will do as illustrations. Here is
one from the *Magnet*:

"Groan!
" 'Shut up, Bunter!'
"Groan!
"Shutting up was not really in Billy Bunter's line. He seldom
shut up, though often requested to do so. On the present awful
occasion the fat Owl of Greyfriars was less inclined than ever
to shut up. And he did not shut up! He groaned, and groaned,
and went on groaning.
"Even groaning did not fully express Bunter's feelings. His
feelings, in fact, were inexpressible.
"There were six of them in the soup! Only one of the six
uttered sounds of woe and lamentation. But that one, William
George Bunter, uttered enough for the whole party and a little
over.
"Harry Wharton & Co. stood in a wrathy and worried group.
They were landed and stranded, diddled, dished and done!" etc.
etc. etc.

Here is one from the *Gem*:

" 'Oh cwumbs!'
" 'Oh gum!'
" 'Oooogh!'
" 'Urrggh!'
"Arthur Augustus sat up dizzily. He grabbed his handkerchief
and pressed it to his damaged nose. Tom Merry sat up, gasping
for breath. They looked at one another.
" 'Bai Jove! This is a go, deah boy!' gurgled Arthur Augustus.
'I have been thwown into quite a fluttah! Oogh! The wottahs!
The wuffians! The feahful outsidahs! Wow!' " etc. etc. etc.

Both of these extracts are entirely typical; you would find
something like them in almost every chapter of every number,

[1] 1945. This is quite incorrect. These stories have been written
throughout the whole period of "Frank Richards" and "Martin Clifford",
who are one and the same person! See articles in *Horizon*, May 1940, and
Summer Pie, summer 1944.

to-day or twenty-five years ago. The first thing that anyone would notice is the extraordinary amount of tautology (the first of these two passages contains a hundred and twenty-five words and could be compressed into about thirty), seemingly designed to spin out the story, but actually playing its part in creating the atmosphere. For the same reason various facetious expressions are repeated over and over again; "wrathy", for instance, is a great favourite, and so is "diddled, dished and done". "Oooogh!", "Grooo!" and "Yaroo!" (stylized cries of pain) recur constantly, and so does "Ha! ha! ha!", always given a line to itself, so that sometimes a quarter of a column or thereabouts consists of "Ha! ha! ha!" The slang ("Go and eat coke!", "What the thump!", "You frabjous ass!", etc., etc.) has never been altered, so that the boys are now using slang which is at least thirty years out of date. In addition, the various nicknames are rubbed in on every possible occasion. Every few lines we are reminded that Harry Wharton & Co. are "the Famous Five", Bunter is always "the fat Owl" or "the Owl of the Remove", Vernon-Smith is always "the Bounder of Greyfriars", Gussy (the Honourable Arthur Augustus D'Arcy) is always "the swell of St. Jim's", and so on and so forth. There is a constant, untiring effort to keep the atmosphere intact and to make sure that every new reader learns immediately who is who. The result has been to make Greyfriars and St. Jim's into an extraordinary little world of their own, a world which cannot be taken seriously by anyone over fifteen, but which at any rate is not easily forgotten. By a debasement of the Dickens technique a series of stereotyped "characters" has been built up, in several cases very successfully. Billy Bunter, for instance, must be one of the best-known figures in English fiction; for the mere number of people who know him he ranks with Sexton Blake, Tarzan, Sherlock Holmes and a handful of characters in Dickens.

Needless to say, these stories are fantastically unlike life at a real public school. They run in cycles of rather differing types, but in general they are the clean-fun, knock-about type of story, with interest centring round horse-play, practical jokes, ragging masters, fights, canings, football, cricket and food. A constantly recurring story is one in which a boy is accused of some misdeed committed by another and is too much of a sportsman to reveal the truth. The "good" boys are "good" in the clean-living Englishman tradition—they keep in hard training, wash behind their ears, never hit below the belt etc., etc.—and by way of contrast there is a series of "bad" boys, Racke, Crooke, Loder and others, whose badness consists in betting, smoking cigarettes and frequenting public-houses. All these boys are constantly on the verge of expulsion, but as it would mean a change of personnel if any boy were actually expelled, no one is ever caught out in any really serious offence. Stealing, for instance, barely enters as a motif. Sex is completely taboo, especially in the form in which it actually arises at public schools. Occasionally girls enter into the stories, and very rarely there is something approaching a mild flirtation, but it is entirely in the spirit of clean fun. A boy and a girl enjoy going for bicycle rides together —that is all it ever amounts to. Kissing, for instance, would be regarded as "soppy". Even the bad boys are presumed to be completely sexless. When the *Gem* and *Magnet* were started, it is probable that there was a deliberate intention to get away from the guilty sex-ridden atmosphere that pervaded so much of the earlier literature for boys. In the 'nineties the *Boy's Own Paper*, for instance, used to have its correspondence columns full of terrifying warnings against masturbation, and books like *St. Winifred's* and *Tom Brown's Schooldays* were heavy with homosexual feeling, though no doubt the authors were not fully aware of it. In the *Gem* and *Magnet* sex simply did not exist as a problem. Religion is also taboo; in the whole thirty years' issue of the two papers the word "God" probably does not occur, except in "God save the King". On the other hand, there has always been a very strong "temperance" strain. Drinking and, by association, smoking are regarded as rather disgraceful even in an adult ("shady" is the usual word), but at the same time as something

irresistibly fascinating, a sort of substitute for sex. In their
moral atmosphere the *Gem* and *Magnet* have a great deal in
common with the Boy Scout movement, which started at about
the same time.

All literature of this kind is partly plagiarism. Sexton Blake,
for instance, started off quite frankly as an imitation of Sherlock
Holmes, and still resembles him fairly strongly; he has hawklike
features, lives in Baker Street, smokes enormously and puts on a
dressing-gown when he wants to think. The *Gem* and *Magnet*
probably owe something to the old school-story writers who
were flourishing when they began, Gunby Hadath, Desmond
Coke and the rest, but they owe more to nineteenth-century
models. In so far as Greyfriars and St. Jim's are like real schools
at all, they are much more like Tom Brown's Rugby than a
modern public school. Neither school has an O.T.C., for instance,
games are not compulsory, and the boys are even allowed to
wear what clothes they like. But without doubt the main origin
of these papers is *Stalky & Co.* This book has had an immense
influence on boys' literature, and it is one of those books which
have a sort of traditional reputation among people who have
never even seen a copy of it. More than once in boys' weekly
papers I have come across a reference to *Stalky & Co.* in which
the word was spelt "Storky". Even the name of the chief comic
among the Greyfriars masters, Mr. Prout, is taken from *Stalky
& Co.*, and so is much of the slang; "jape", "merry", "giddy",
"bizney" (business), "frabjous", "don't" for "doesn't"—all of
them out of date even when *Gem* and *Magnet* started. There are
also traces of earlier origins. The name "Greyfriars" is probably
taken from Thackeray, and Gosling, the school porter in the
Magnet, talks in an imitation of Dickens's dialect.

With all this, the supposed "glamour" of public-school life
is played for all it is worth. There is all the usual paraphernalia—
lock-up, roll-call, house matches, fagging, prefects, cosy teas
round the study fire, etc., etc.—and constant reference to the
"old school", the "old grey stones" (both schools were founded

in the early sixteenth century), the "team spirit" of the "Grey-friars men". As for the snob-appeal, it is completely shameless. Each school has a titled boy or two whose titles are constantly thrust in the reader's face; other boys have the names of well-known aristocratic families, Talbot, Manners, Lowther. We are for ever being reminded that Gussy is the Honourable Arthur A. D'Arcy, son of Lord Eastwood, that Jack Blake is heir to "broad acres", that Hurree Jamset Ram Singh (nicknamed Inky) is the Nabob of Bhanipur, that Vernon-Smith's father is a millionaire. Till recently the illustrations in both papers always depicted the boys in clothes imitated from those of Eton; in the last few years Greyfriars has changed over to blazers and flannel trousers, but St. Jim's still sticks to the Eton jacket, and Gussy sticks to his top-hat. In the school magazine which appears every week as part of the *Magnet*, Harry Wharton writes an article discussing the pocket-money received by the "fellows in the Remove", and reveals that some of them get as much as five pounds a week! This kind of thing is a perfectly deliberate incitement to wealth-fantasy. And here it is worth noticing a rather curious fact, and that is that the school story is a thing peculiar to England. So far as I know, there are extremely few school stories in foreign languages. The reason, obviously, is that in England education is mainly a matter of status. The most definite dividing line between the petite-bourgeoisie and the working class is that the former pay for their education, and within the bourgeoisie there is another unbridgeable gulf between the "public" school and the "private" school. It is quite clear that there are tens and scores of thousands of people to whom every detail of life at a "posh" public school is wildly thrilling and romantic. They happen to be outside that mystic world of quadrangles and house-colours, but they can yearn after it, day-dream about it, live mentally in it for hours at a stretch. The question is, Who are these people? Who reads the *Gem* and *Magnet*?

Obviously one can never be quite certain about this kind of thing All I can say from my own observation is this. Boys who are likely to go to public schools themselves generally read the *Gem* and *Magnet*, but they nearly always stop reading them when they are about twelve; they may continue for another year from force of habit, but by that time they have ceased to take them seriously. On the other hand, the boys at very cheap private schools, the schools that are designed for people who can't afford a public school but consider the Council schools "common", continue reading the *Gem* and *Magnet* for several years longer. A few years ago I was a teacher at two of these schools myself. I found that not only did virtually all the boys read the *Gem* and *Magnet*, but that they were still taking them fairly seriously when they were fifteen or even sixteen. These boys were the sons of shop-keepers, office employees and small business and professional men, and obviously it is this class that the *Gem* and *Magnet* are aimed at. But they are certainly read by working-class boys as well. They are generally on sale in the poorest quarters of big towns, and I have known them to be read by boys whom one might expect to be completely immune from public-school "glamour". I have seen a young coal-miner, for instance, a lad who had already worked a year or two underground, eagerly reading the *Gem*. Recently I offered a batch of English papers to some British legionaries of the French Foreign Legion in North Africa; they picked out the *Gem* and *Magnet* first. Both papers are much read by girls,[1] and the Pen Pals department of the *Gem* shows that it is read in every corner of the British Empire, by Australians, Canadians, Palestine Jews, Malays, Arabs, Straits Chinese, etc., etc. The editors evidently expect their readers to be aged round about fourteen, and the advertisements (milk chocolate, postage stamps, water pistols, blushing cured, home conjuring tricks, itching powder, the Phine Phun Ring which runs a needle into your friend's hand, etc., etc.) indicate roughly the same age; there are also the Admiralty

---

[1] There are several corresponding girls' papers. The *Schoolgirl* is companion-paper to the *Magnet* and has stories by "Hilda Richards". The characters are interchangeable to some extent. Bessie Bunter, Billy Bunter's sister, figures in the *Schoolgirl*.

vertisements, however, which call for youths between seven-
n and twenty-two. And there is no question that these papers
: also read by adults. It is quite common for people to write
the editor and say that they have read every number of the
m or *Magnet* for the past thirty years. Here, for instance, is a
ter from a lady in Salisbury:

"I can say of your splendid yarns of Harry Wharton & Co. of
:eyfriars, that they never fail to reach a high standard. With-
t doubt they are the finest stories of their type on the market
-day, which is saying a good deal. They seem to bring you face
face with Nature. I have taken the *Magnet* from the start, and
ve followed the adventures of Harry Wharton & Co. with rapt
:erest. I have no sons, but two daughters, and there's always a
sh to be the first to read the grand old paper. My husband, too,
s a staunch reader of the *Magnet* until he was suddenly taken
·ay from us."

It is well worth getting hold of some copies of the *Gem* and
agnet, especially the *Gem*, simply to have a look at the corre-
ondence columns. What is truly startling is the intense interest
th which the pettiest details of life at Greyfriars and St. Jim's
: followed up. Here, for instance, are a few of the questions
it in by readers:

"What age is Dick Roylance?" "How old is St. Jim's?" "Can
u give me a list of the Shell and their studies?" "How much
d D'Arcy's monocle cost?" "How is it that fellows like Crooke
: in the Shell and decent fellows like yourself are only in the
urth?" "What are the Form captain's three chief duties?"
Who is the chemistry master at St. Jim's?" (From a girl) "Where
St. Jim's situated? *Could* you tell me how to get there, as I
uld love to see the building? Are you boys just 'phoneys', as I
ink you are?"

It is clear that many of the boys and girls who write these
ters are living a complete fantasy-life. Sometimes a boy will
ite, for instance, giving his age, height, weight, chest and bicep
:asurements and asking which member of the Shell or Fourth
·rm he most exactly resembles. The demand for a list of the
dies on the Shell passage, with an exact account of who

lives in each, is a very common one. The editors, of course,
everything in their power to keep up the illusion. In the *G*
Jack Blake is supposed to write the answers to corresponden
and in the *Magnet* a couple of pages is always given up to t
school magazine (the *Greyfriars Herald*, edited by Har
Wharton), and there is another page in which one or oth
character is written up each week. The stories run in cycles, tw
or three characters being kept in the foreground for seve:
weeks at a time. First there will be a series of rollicking adventu
stories, featuring the Famous Five and Billy Bunter; then a r
of stories turning on mistaken identity, with Wibley (the make-
wizard) in the star part; then a run of more serious stories
which Vernon-Smith is trembling on the verge of expulsic
And here one comes upon the real secret of the *Gem* and *Magr*
and the probable reason why they continue to be read in sp
of their obvious out-of-dateness.

It is that the characters are so carefully graded as to gi
almost every type of reader a character he can identify hims
with. Most boys' papers aim at doing this, hence the bo
assistant (Sexton Blake's Tinker, Nelson Lee's Nipper, et
who usually accompanies the explorer, detective or what-not
his adventures. But in these cases there is only one boy, a
usually it is much the same type of boy. In the *Gem* and *Magr*
there is a model for nearly everybody. There is the norm
athletic, high-spirited boy (Tom Merry, Jack Blake, Fra
Nugent), a slightly rowdier version of this type (Bob Cherry)
more aristocratic version (Talbot, Manners), a quieter, mc
serious version (Harry Wharton), and a stolid, "bulldo
version (Johnny Bull). Then there is the reckless, dare-de
type of boy (Vernon-Smith), the definitely "clever", studio
boy (Mark Linley, Dick Penfold), and the eccentric boy who
not good at games but possesses some special talent (Skinr
Wibley). And there is the scholarship-boy (Tom Redwing),
important figure in this class of story because he makes it possil
for boys from very poor homes to project themselves into t

blic-school atmosphere. In addition there are Australian, Irish,
'elsh, Manx, Yorkshire and Lancashire boys to play upon local
triotism. But the subtlety of characterization goes deeper than
is. If one studies the correspondence columns one sees that
ere is probably *no* character in the *Gem* and *Magnet* whom
me or other reader does not identify with, except the out-and-
t comics, Coker, Billy Bunter, Fisher T. Fish (the money-
ubbing American boy) and, of course, the masters. Bunter,
ough in his origin he probably owed something to the fat boy
Pickwick, is a real creation. His tight trousers against which
ots and canes are constantly thudding, his astuteness in search
food, his postal order which never turns up, have made him
mous wherever the Union Jack waves. But he is not a subject
r day-dreams. On the other hand, another seeming figure of
n, Gussy (the Honourable Arthur A. D'Arcy, "the swell of St.
m's"), is evidently much admired. Like everything else in the
em and *Magnet*, Gussy is at least thirty years out of date. He
the "knut" of the early twentieth century or even the "masher"
the 'nineties ("Bai Jove, deah boy!" and "Weally, I shall be
liged to give you a feahful thwashin'!'"), the monocled idiot
ho made good on the fields of Mons and Le Cateau. And his
ident popularity goes to show how deep the snob-appeal of
is type is. English people are extremely fond of the titled ass
f. Lord Peter Wimsey) who always turns up trumps in the
oment of emergency. Here is a letter from one of Gussy's girl
lmirers:

"I think you're too hard on Gussy. I wonder he's still in
istence, the way you treat him. He's my hero. Did you know
write lyrics? How's this—to the tune of 'Goody Goody'?

"Gonna get my gas-mask, join the A.R.P.
'Cos I'm wise to all those bombs you drop on me.
Gonna dig myself a trench
Inside the garden fence;
Gonna seal my windows up with tin
So the tear gas can't get in;

Gonna park my cannon right outside the kerb
With a note to Adolf Hitler: 'Don't disturb!'
And if I never fall in Nazi hands
That's soon enough for me
Gonna get my gas-mask, join the A.R.P.

"PS.—Do you get on well with girls?"

I quote this in full because (dated April 1939) it is interesti
as being probably the earliest mention of Hitler in the *Gem*.
the *Gem* there is also a heroic fat boy, Fatty Wynn, as a set-
against Bunter. Vernon-Smith, "the Bounder of the Remove",
Byronic character, always on the verge of the sack, is anoth
great favourite. And even some of the cads probably have th
following. Loder, for instance, "the rotter of the Sixth", is a ca
but he is also a highbrow and given to saying sarcastic thin
about football and the team spirit. The boys of the Remove on
think him all the more of a cad for this, but a certain type of b
would probably identify with him. Even Racke, Crooke & C
are probably admired by small boys who think it diabolical
wicked to smoke cigarettes. (A frequent question in the corr
spondence column: "What brand of cigarettes does Rac
smoke?")

Naturally the politics of the *Gem* and *Magnet* are Conservativ
but in a completely pre-1914 style, with no Fascist tinge. I
reality their basic political assumptions are two: nothing ev
changes, and foreigners are funny. In the *Gem* of 1939 Frenc
men are still Froggies and Italians are still Dagoes. Mossoo, t
French master at Greyfriars, is the usual comic-paper Frog, wi
pointed beard, pegtop trousers, etc. Inky, the Indian boy, thoug
a rajah, and therefore possessing snob-appeal, is also the com
babu of the *Punch* tradition. (" 'The rowfulness is not the prop
caper, my esteemed Bob,' said Inky. 'Let dogs delight in tl
barkfulness and bitefulness, but the soft answer is the crack
pitcher that goes longest to a bird in the bush, as the Englis
proverb remarks.' ") Fisher T. Fish is the old-style stage Yank
(" 'Waal, I guess' ", etc.) dating from a period of Anglo-America

jealousy. Wun Lung, the Chinese boy (he has rather faded out of late, no doubt because some of the *Magnet's* readers are Straits Chinese), is the nineteenth-century pantomime China-man, with saucer-shaped hat, pigtail and pidgin-English. The assumption all along is not only that foreigners are comics who are put there for us to laugh at, but that they can be classified in much the same way as insects. That is why in all boys' papers, not only the *Gem* and *Magnet*, a Chinese is invariably portrayed with a pigtail. It is the thing you recognize him by, like the Frenchman's beard or the Italian's barrel-organ. In papers of this kind it occasionally happens that when the setting of a story is in a foreign country some attempt is made to describe the natives as individual human beings, but as a rule it is assumed that foreigners of any one race are all alike and will conform more or less exactly to the following patterns:

FRENCHMAN: Excitable. Wears beard, gesticulates wildly.
SPANIARD, MEXICAN, etc.: Sinister, treacherous.
ARAB, AFGHAN, etc.: Sinister, treacherous.
CHINESE: Sinister, treacherous. Wears pigtail.
ITALIAN: Excitable. Grinds barrel-organ or carries stiletto
SWEDE, DANE, etc.: Kind-hearted, stupid.
NEGRO: Comic, very faithful.

The working classes only enter into the *Gem* and *Magnet* as comics or semi-villains (race-course touts, etc.). As for class-friction, trade unionism, strikes, slumps, unemployment, Fascism and civil war—not a mention. Somewhere or other in the thirty years' issue of the two papers you might perhaps find the word "Socialism", but you would have to look a long time for it. If the Russian Revolution is anywhere referred to, it will be indirectly, in the word "Bolshy" (meaning a person of violent disagreeable habits). Hitler and the Nazis are just beginning to make their appearance, in the sort of reference I quoted above. The war-crisis of September 1938 made just enough impression to produce a story in which Mr. Vernon-Smith, the Bounder's

millionaire father, cashed in on the general panic by buying up
country houses in order to sell them to "crisis scuttlers". But
that is probably as near to noticing the European situation as the
Gem and *Magnet* will come, until the war actually starts.[1] That
does not mean that these papers are unpatriotic—quite the
contrary! Throughout the Great War the *Gem* and *Magnet* were
perhaps the most consistently and cheerfully patriotic papers in
England. Almost every week the boys caught a spy or pushed a
conchy into the army, and during the rationing period "EAT LESS
BREAD" was printed in large type on every page. But their
patriotism has nothing whatever to do with power-politics or
"idealogical" warfare. It is more akin to family loyalty, and
actually it gives one a valuable clue to the attitude of ordinary
people, especially the huge untouched block of the middle class
and the better-off working class. These people are patriotic to
the middle of their bones, but they do not feel that what happens
in foreign countries is any of their business. When England is in
danger they rally to its defence as a matter of course, but in
between-times they are not interested. After all, England is always
in the right and England always wins, so why worry? It is an
attitude that has been shaken during the past twenty years, but
not so deeply as is sometimes supposed. Failure to understand
it is one of the reasons why Left-Wing political parties are
seldom able to produce an acceptable foreign policy.

The mental world of the *Gem* and *Magnet*, therefore, is
something like this:

The year is 1910—or 1940, but it is all the same. You are at
Greyfriars, a rosy-cheeked boy of fourteen in posh tailor-made
clothes, sitting down to tea in your study on the Remove passage
after an exciting game of football which was won by an odd goal
in the last half-minute. There is a cosy fire in the study, and
outside the wind is whistling. The ivy clusters thickly round the

---

[1] This was written some months before the outbreak of war. Up to the
end of September 1939 no mention of the war has appeared in either
paper.

old grey stones. The King is on his throne and the pound is worth a pound. Over in Europe the comic foreigners are jabbering and gesticulating, but the grim grey battleships of the British Fleet are steaming up the Channel and at the outposts of Empire the monocled Englishmen are holding the niggers at bay. Lord Mauleverer has just got another fiver and we are all settling down to a tremendous tea of sausages, sardines, crumpets, potted meat, jam and doughnuts. After tea we shall sit round the study fire having a good laugh at Billy Bunter and discussing the team for next week's match against Rookwood. Everything is safe, solid and unquestionable. Everything will be the same for ever and ever. That approximately is the atmosphere.

But now turn from the *Gem* and *Magnet* to the more up-to-date papers which have appeared since the Great War. The truly significant thing is that they have more points of resemblance to the *Gem* and *Magnet* than points of difference. But it is better to consider the differences first.

There are eight of these newer papers, the *Modern Boy*, *Triumph*, *Champion*, *Wizard*, *Rover*, *Skipper*, *Hotspur* and *Adventure*. All of these have appeared since the Great War, but except for the *Modern Boy* none of them is less than five years old. Two papers which ought also to be mentioned briefly here, though they are not strictly in the same class as the rest, are the *Detective Weekly* and the *Thriller*, both owned by the Amalgamated Press. The *Detective Weekly* has taken over Sexton Blake. Both of these papers admit a certain amount of sex-interest into their stories, and though certainly read by boys, they are not aimed at them exclusively. All the others are boys' papers pure and simple, and they are sufficiently alike to be considered together. There does not seem to be any notable difference between Thomson's publications and those of the Amalgamated Press.

As soon as one looks at these papers one sees their technical superiority to the *Gem* and *Magnet*. To begin with, they have the great advantage of not being written entirely by one person.

Instead of one long complete story, a number of the *Wizard* or *Hotspur* consists of half a dozen or more serials, none of which goes on for ever. Consequently there is far more variety and far less padding, and none of the tiresome stylization and facetiousness of the *Gem* and *Magnet*. Look at these two extracts, for example:

"Billy Bunter groaned.

"A quarter of an hour had elapsed out of the two hours that Bunter was booked for extra French.

"In a quarter of an hour there were only fifteen minutes! But every one of those minutes seemed inordinately long to Bunter. They seemed to crawl by like tired snails.

"Looking at the clock in Class-room No. 10 the fat Owl could hardly believe that only fifteen minutes had passed. It seemed more like fifteen hours, if not fifteen days!

"Other fellows were in extra French as well as Bunter. They did not matter. Bunter did!" (the *Magnet*).

"After a terrible climb, hacking out handholds in the smooth ice every step of the way up, Sergeant Lionheart Logan of the Mounties was now clinging like a human fly to the face of an icy cliff, as smooth and treacherous as a giant pane of glass.

"An Arctic blizzard, in all its fury, was buffeting his body, driving the blinding snow into his face, seeking to tear his fingers loose from their handholds and dash him to death on the jagged boulders which lay at the foot of the cliff a hundred feet below.

"Crouching among those boulders were eleven villainous trappers who had done their best to shoot down Lionheart and his companion, Constable Jim Rogers—until the blizzard had blotted the two Mounties out of sight from below" (the *Wizard*).

The second extract gets you some distance with the story, the first takes a hundred words to tell you that Bunter is in the detention class. Moreover, by not concentrating on school stories (in point of numbers the school story slightly predominates in all these papers, except the *Thriller* and *Detective Weekly*), the *Wizard*, *Hotspur*, etc., have far greater opportunities for sensationalism. Merely looking at the cover illustrations of the papers which I have on the table in front of me, here are some of the things I see. On one a cowboy is clinging by his toes to the wing of an aeroplane in mid-air and shooting down another aeroplane with his revolver. On another a Chinese is swimming for his life down a sewer with a swarm of ravenous-looking rats swimming after him. On another an engineer is lighting a stick of dynamite while a steel robot feels for him with its claws. On another a man in airman's costume is fighting barehanded against a rat somewhat larger than a donkey. On another a nearly naked man of terrific muscular development has just seized a lion by the tail and flung it thirty yards over the wall of an arena, with the words, "Take back your blooming lion!" Clearly no school story can compete with this kind of thing. From time to time the school buildings may catch fire or the French master may turn out to be the head of an international anarchist gang, but in a general way the interest must centre round cricket, school rivalries, practical jokes, etc. There is not much room for bombs, death-rays, sub-machine guns, aeroplanes, mustangs, octopuses, grizzly bears or gangsters.

Examination of a large number of these papers shows that, putting aside school stories, the favourite subjects are Wild West, Frozen North, Foreign Legion, crime (always from the detective's angle), the Great War (Air Force or Secret Service, not the infantry), the Tarzan motif in varying forms, professional football, tropical exploration, historical romance (Robin Hood, Cavaliers and Roundheads, etc.) and scientific invention. The Wild West still leads, at any rate as a setting, though the Red Indian seems to be fading out. The one theme that is really new is the scientific one. Death-rays, Martians, invisible men, robots, helicopters and interplanetary rockets figure largely; here and there there are even far-off rumours of psychotherapy and ductless glands. Whereas the *Gem* and *Magnet* derive from Dickens and Kipling, the *Wizard, Champion, Modern Boy,* etc., owe a great deal to H. G. Wells, who, rather than Jules Verne, is the father of "Scientifiction". Naturally it is the magical

Martian aspect of science that is most exploited, but one or two papers include serious articles on scientific subjects, besides quantities of informative snippets. (Examples: "A Kauri tree in Queensland, Australia, is over 12,000 years old"; "Nearly 50,000 thunderstorms occur every day"; "Helium gas costs £1 per 1000 cubic feet"; "There are over 500 varieties of spiders in Great Britain"; "London firemen use 14,000,000 gallons of water annually," etc., etc.) There is a marked advance in intellectual curiosity and, on the whole, in the demand made on the reader's attention. In practice the *Gem* and *Magnet* and the post-war papers are read by much the same public, but the mental age aimed at seems to have risen by a year or two years—an improvement probably corresponding to the improvement in elementary education since 1909.

The other thing that has emerged in the post-war boys' papers, though not to anything like the extent one would expect, is bully-worship and the cult of violence.

If one compares the *Gem* and *Magnet* with a genuinely modern paper, the thing that immediately strikes one is the absence of the leader-principle. There is no central dominating character; instead there are fifteen or twenty characters, all more or less on an equality, with whom readers of different types can identify. In the more modern papers this is not usually the case. Instead of identifying with a schoolboy of more or less his own age, the reader of the *Skipper*, *Hotspur*, etc., is led to identify with a G-man, with a Foreign Legionary, with some variant of Tarzan, with an air ace, a master spy, an explorer, a pugilist—at any rate with some single all-powerful character who dominates everyone about him and whose usual method of solving any problem is a sock on the jaw. This character is intended as a superman, and as physical strength is the form of power that boys can best understand, he is usually a sort of human gorilla; in the Tarzan type of story he is sometimes actually a giant, eight or ten feet high. At the same time the scenes of violence in nearly all these stories are remarkably harmless and unconvincing. There is a great difference in tone between even the most bloodthirsty English paper and the threepenny Yank Mags, *Fight Stories*, *Action Stories*, etc. (not strictly boys' papers, but largely read by boys). In the Yank Mags you get real blood-lust, really gory descriptions of the all-in, jump-on-his-testicles style fighting, written in a jargon that has been perfected by people who brood endlessly on violence. A paper like *Fight Stories*, for instance, would have very little appeal except to sadists and masochists. You can see the comparative gentleness of the English civilization by the amateurish way in which prize-fighting is always described in the boys' weeklies. There is no specialized vocabulary. Look at these four extracts, two English, two American:

"When the gong sounded, both men were breathing heavily and each had great red marks on his chest. Bill's chin was bleeding, and Ben had a cut over his right eye.

"Into their corners they sank, but when the gong clanged again they were up swiftly, and they went like tigers at each other" (*Rover*).

"He walked in stolidly and smashed a clublike right to my face. Blood spattered and I went back on my heels, but surged in and ripped my right under the heart. Another right smashed full on Ben's already battered mouth, and, spitting out the fragments of a tooth, he crashed a flailing left to my body" (*Fight Stories*).

"It was amazing to watch the Black Panther at work. His muscles rippled and slid under his dark skin. There was all the power and grace of a giant cat in his swift and terrible onslaught.

"He volleyed blows with a bewildering speed for so huge a fellow. In a moment Ben was simply blocking with his gloves as well as he could. Ben was really a past-master of defence. He had many fine victories behind him. But the Negro's rights and lefts crashed through openings that hardly any other fighter could have found" (*Wizard*).

"Haymakers which packed the bludgeoning weight of forest monarchs crashing down under the ax hurled into the bodies of the two heavies as they swapped punches" (*Fight Stories*).

Notice how much more knowledgeable the American extracts sound. They are written for devotees of the prize-ring, the others are not. Also, it ought to be emphasized that on its level the moral code of the English boys' papers is a decent one. Crime and dishonesty are never held up to admiration, there is none of the cynicism and corruption of the American gangster story. The huge sale of the Yank Mags in England shows that there is a demand for that kind of thing, but very few English writers seem able to produce it. When hatred of Hitler became a major emotion in America, it was interesting to see how promptly "anti-Fascism" was adapted to pornographic purposes by the editors of the Yank Mags. One magazine which I have in front of me is given up to a long, complete story, "When Hell Came to America", in which the agents of a "blood-maddened European dictator" are trying to conquer the U.S.A. with death-rays and invisible aeroplanes. There is the frankest appeal to sadism, scenes in which the Nazis tie bombs to women's backs and fling them off heights to watch them blown to pieces in mid-air, others in which they tie naked girls together by their hair and prod them with knives to make them dance, etc., etc. The editor comments solemnly on all this, and uses it as a plea for tightening up restrictions against immigrants. On another page of the same paper: "LIVES OF THE HOTCHA CHORUS GIRLS. Reveals all the intimate secrets and fascinating pastimes of the famous Broadway Hotcha girls. NOTHING IS OMITTED. Price 10c." "HOW TO LOVE. 10c." "FRENCH PHOTO RING. 25c." "NAUGHTY NUDIES TRANSFERS. From the outside of the glass you see a beautiful girl, innocently dressed. Turn it around and look through the glass and oh! what a difference! Set of 3 transfers 25c.," etc., etc., etc. There is nothing at all like this in any English paper likely to be read by boys. But the process of Americanization is going on all the same. The American ideal, the "he-man", the "tough guy", the gorilla who puts everything right by socking everybody else on the jaw, now figures in probably a majority of boys' papers. In one serial now running in the *Skipper* he is always portrayed ominously enough, swinging a rubber truncheon.

The development of the *Wizard, Hotspur*, etc., as against the earlier boys' papers, boils down to this: better technique, more scientific interest, more bloodshed, more leader-worship. But, after all, it is the *lack* of development that is the really striking thing.

To begin with, there is no political development whatever. The world of the *Skipper* and the *Champion* is still the pre-1914 world of the *Magnet* and the *Gem*. The Wild West story, for instance, with its cattle-rustlers, lynch-law and other paraphernalia belonging to the 'eighties, is a curiously archaic thing. It is worth noticing that in papers of this type it is always taken for granted that adventures only happen at the ends of the earth, in tropical forests, in Arctic wastes, in African deserts, on Western prairies, in Chinese opium dens—everywhere in fact, except the places where things really *do* happen. That is a belief dating from thirty or forty years ago, when the new continents were in process of being opened up. Nowadays, of course, if you really want adventure, the place to look for it is in Europe. But apart from the picturesque side of the Great War, contemporary history is carefully excluded. And except that Americans are now admired instead of being laughed at, foreigners are exactly the same figures of fun that they always were. If a Chinese character appears, he is still the sinister pigtailed opium-smuggler of Sax Rohmer; no indication that things have been happening in China since 1912—no indication that a war is going on there, for instance. If a Spaniard appears, he is still a "dago" or "greaser" who rolls cigarettes and stabs people in the back; no indication that things have been happening in Spain. Hitler and the Nazis have not yet appeared, or are barely making their appearance. There will be plenty about them in a little while, but it will be from a strictly patriotic angle (Britain *versus* Germany), with the real meaning of the struggle kept out of sight as much as possible. As for the Russian Revolution, it is extremely difficult to find any reference to it in any of these papers. When Russia is mentioned at all it is usually in an information snippet (example: "There are 29,000 centenarians in the U.S.S.R."), and any reference to the Revolution is indirect and twenty years out of date. In one story in the *Rover*, for instance, somebody has a tame bear, and as it is a Russian bear, it is nicknamed Trotsky—obviously an echo of the 1917–23 period and not of recent controversies. The clock has stopped at 1910. Britannia rules the waves, and no one has heard of slumps, booms, unemployment, dictatorships, purges or concentration camps.

And in social outlook there is hardly any advance. The snobbishness is somewhat less open than in the *Gem* and *Magnet* —that is the most one can possibly say. To begin with, the school story, always partly dependent on snob-appeal, is by no means eliminated. Every number of a boys' paper includes at least one school story, these stories slightly outnumbering the Wild Westerns. The very elaborate fantasy-life of the *Gem* and *Magnet* is not imitated and there is more emphasis on extraneous adventure, but the social atmosphere (old grey stones) is much the same. When a new school is introduced at the beginning of a story we are often told in just those words that "it was a very posh school". From time to time a story appears which is ostensibly directed *against* snobbery. The scholarship-boy (cf. Tom Redwing in the *Magnet*) makes fairly frequent appearances, and what is essentially the same theme is sometimes presented in this form; there is great rivalry between two schools, one of which considers itself more "posh" than the other, and there are fights, practical jokes, football matches, etc., always ending in the discomfiture of the snobs. If one glances very superficially at some of these stories it is possible to imagine that a democratic spirit has crept into the boys' weeklies, but when one looks more closely one sees that they merely reflect the bitter jealousies that exist within the white-collar class. Their real function is to allow the boy who goes to a cheap private school (*not* a Council school) to feel that his school is just as "posh" in the sight of God as Winchester or Eton. The sentiment of school loyalty

("We're better than the fellows down the road"), a thing almost unknown to the real working class, is still kept up. As these stories are written by many different hands, they do, of course, vary a good deal in tone. Some are reasonably free from snobbishness, in others money and pedigree are exploited even more shamelessly than in the *Gem* and *Magnet*. In one that I came across an actual *majority* of the boys mentioned were titled.

Where working-class characters appear, it is usually either as comics (jokes about tramps, convicts, etc.), or as prize-fighters, acrobats, cowboys, professional footballers and Foreign Legionaries—in other words, as adventurers. There is no facing of the facts about working-class life, or, indeed, about *working* life of any description. Very occasionally one may come across a realistic description of, say, work in a coal-mine, but in all probability it will only be there as the background of some lurid adventure. In any case the central character is not likely to be a coal-miner. Nearly all the time the boy who reads these papers—in nine cases out of ten a boy who is going to spend his life working in a shop, in a factory or in some subordinate job in an office—is led to identify with people in positions of command, above all with people who are never troubled by shortage of money. The Lord Peter Wimsey figure, the seeming idiot who drawls and wears a monocle but is always to the fore in moments of danger, turns up over and over again. (This character is a great favourite in Secret Service stories.) And, as usual, the heroic characters all have to talk B.B.C.; they may talk Scottish or Irish or American, but no one in a star part is ever permitted to drop an aitch. Here it is worth comparing the social atmosphere of the boys' weeklies with that of the women's weeklies, the *Oracle*, the *Family Star*, *Peg's Paper*, etc.

The women's papers are aimed at an older public and are read for the most part by girls who are working for a living. Consequently they are on the surface much more realistic. It is taken for granted, for example, that nearly everyone has to live in a big town and work at a more or less dull job. Sex, so far from being taboo, is *the* subject. The short, complete stories, the special feature of these papers, are generally of the "came the dawn" type: the heroine narrowly escapes losing her "boy" to a designing rival, or the "boy" loses his job and has to postpone marriage, but presently gets a better job. The changeling-fantasy (a girl brought up in a poor home is "really" the child of rich parents) is another favourite. Where sensationalism comes in, usually in the serials, it arises out of the more domestic type of crime, such as bigamy, forgery or sometimes murder; no Martians, death-rays or international anarchist gangs. These papers are at any rate aiming at credibility, and they have a link with real life in their correspondence columns, where genuine problems are being discussed. Ruby M. Ayres's column of advice in the *Oracle*, for instance, is extremely sensible and well written. And yet the world of the *Oracle* and *Peg's Paper* is a pure fantasy-world. It is the same fantasy all the time; pretending to be richer than you are. The chief impression that one carries away from almost every story in these papers is of a frightful, overwhelming "refinement". Ostensibly the characters are working-class people, but their habits, the interiors of their houses, their clothes, their outlook and, above all, their speech are entirely middle class. They are all living at several pounds a week above their income. And needless to say, that is just the impression that is intended. The idea is to give the bored factory-girl or worn-out mother of five a dream-life in which she pictures herself—not actually as a duchess (that convention has gone out) but as, say, the wife of a bank-manager. Not only is a five-to-six-pound-a-week standard of life set up as the ideal, but it is tacitly assumed that that is how working-class people really *do* live. The major facts are simply not faced. It is admitted, for instance, that people some-times lose their jobs; but then the dark clouds roll away and they get better jobs instead. No mention of unemployment as some-thing permanent and inevitable, no mention of the dole, no mention of trade unionism. No suggestion anywhere that there can be anything wrong with the system *as a system*; there are

only individual misfortunes, which are generally due to somebody's wickedness and can in any case be put right in the last
chapter. Always the dark clouds roll away, the kind employer
raises Alfred's wages, and there are jobs for everybody except
the drunks. It is still the world of the *Wizard* and the *Gem*,
except that there are orange-blossoms instead of machine-
guns.

The outlook inculcated by all these papers is that of a rather
exceptionally stupid member of the Navy League in the year
1910. Yes, it may be said, but what does it matter? And in any
case, what else do you expect?

Of course no one in his senses would want to turn the so-called
penny dreadful into a realistic novel or a Socialist tract. An
adventure story must of its nature be more or less remote from
real life. But, as I have tried to make clear, the unreality of the
Wizard and the *Gem* is not so artless as it looks. These papers
exist because of a specialized demand, because boys at certain
ages find it necessary to read about Martians, death-rays, grizzly
bears and gangsters. They get what they are looking for, but
they get it wrapped up in the illusions which their future em-
ployers think suitable for them. To what extent people draw
their ideas from fiction is disputable. Personally I believe that
most people are influenced far more than they would care to
admit by novels, serial stories, films and so forth, and that from
this point of view the worst books are often the most important,
because they are usually the ones that are read earliest in life. It
is probable that many people who would consider themselves
extremely sophisticated and "advanced" are actually carrying
through life an imaginative background which they acquired in
childhood from (for instance) Sapper and Ian Hay. If that is so,
the boys' twopenny weeklies are of the deepest importance.
Here is the stuff that is read somewhere between the ages of
twelve and eighteen by a very large proportion, perhaps an
actual majority, of English boys, including many who will never
read anything else except newspapers; and along with it they are

absorbing a set of beliefs which would be regarded as hopelessly
out of date in the Central Office of the Conservative Party. All
the better because it is done indirectly, there is being pumped
into them the conviction that the major problems of our time do
not exist, that there is nothing wrong with *laissez-faire* capitalism,
that foreigners are unimportant comics and that the British
Empire is a sort of charity-concern which will last for ever.
Considering who owns these papers, it is difficult to believe that
this is unintentional. Of the twelve papers I have been discussing
(i.e. twelve including the *Thriller* and *Detective Weekly*) seven
are the property of the Amalgamated Press, which is one of the
biggest press-combines in the world and controls more than a
hundred different papers. The *Gem* and *Magnet*, therefore, are
closely linked up with the *Daily Telegraph* and the *Financial
Times*. This in itself would be enough to rouse certain suspicions,
even if it were not obvious that the stories in the boys' weeklies
are politically vetted. So it appears that if you feel the need of a
fantasy-life in which you travel to Mars and fight lions barehanded (and what boy doesn't?), you can only have it by deliver-
ing yourself over, mentally, to people like Lord Camrose. For
there is no competition. Throughout the whole of this run of
papers the differences are negligible, and on this level no others
exist. This raises the question, why is there no such thing as a
left-wing boys' paper?

At first glance such an idea merely makes one slightly sick.
It is so horribly easy to imagine what a left-wing boys' paper
would be like, if it existed. I remember in 1920 or 1921 some
optimistic person handing round Communist tracts among a
crowd of public-school boys. The tract I received was of the
question-and-answer kind:

Q. "Can a Boy Communist be a Boy Scout, Comrade?"
A. "No, Comrade."
Q. "Why, Comrade?"
A. "Because, Comrade, a Boy Scout must salute the Union
Jack, which is the symbol of tyranny and oppression." Etc. etc.

Now, suppose that at this moment somebody started a left-wing paper deliberately aimed at boys of twelve or fourteen. I do not suggest that the whole of its contents would be exactly like the tract I have quoted above, but does anyone doubt that they would be *something* like it? Inevitably such a paper would either consist of dreary uplift or it would be under Communist influence and given over to adulation of Soviet Russia; in either case no normal boy would ever look at it. Highbrow literature apart, the whole of the existing left-wing Press, in so far as it is at all vigorously "left", is one long tract. The one Socialist paper in England which could live a week on its merits *as a paper* is the *Daily Herald*: and how much Socialism is there in the *Daily Herald*? At this moment, therefore, a paper with a "left" slant and at the same time likely to have an appeal to ordinary boys in their teens is something almost beyond hoping for.

But it does not follow that it is impossible. There is no clear reason why every adventure story should necessarily be mixed up with snobbishness and gutter patriotism. For, after all, the stories in the *Hotspur* and the *Modern Boy* are not Conservative tracts; they are merely adventure stories with a Conservative bias. It is fairly easy to imagine the process being reversed. It is possible, for instance, to imagine a paper as thrilling and lively as the *Hotspur*, but with subject-matter and "ideology" a little more up to date. It is even possible (though this raises other difficulties) to imagine a women's paper at the same literary level as the *Oracle*, dealing in approximately the same kind of story, but taking rather more account of the realities of working-class life. Such things have been done before, though not in England. In the last years of the Spanish monarchy there was a large output in Spain of left-wing novelettes, some of them evidently of anarchist origin. Unfortunately at the time when they were appearing I did not see their social significance, and I lost the collection of them that I had, but no doubt copies would still be procurable. In get-up and style of story they were very similar to the English fourpenny novelette, except that their inspiration was "left". If, for instance, a story described police pursuing anarchists through the mountains, it would be from the point of view of the anarchist and not of the police. An example nearer to hand is the Soviet film *Chapaiev*, which has been shown a number of times in London. Technically, by the standards of the time when it was made, *Chapaiev* is a first-rate film, but mentally, in spite of the unfamiliar Russian background, it is not so very remote from Hollywood. The one thing that lifts it out of the ordinary is the remarkable performance by the actor who takes the part of the White officer (the fat one)—a performance which looks very like an inspired piece of gagging. Otherwise the atmosphere is familiar. All the usual paraphernalia is there—heroic fight against odds, escape at the last moment, shots of galloping horses, love interest, comic relief. The film is in fact a fairly ordinary one, except that its tendency is "left". In a Hollywood film of the Russian Civil War the Whites would probably be angels and the Reds demons. In the Russian version the Reds are angels and the Whites demons. That is also a lie, but, taking the long view, it is a less pernicious lie than the other.

Here several difficult problems present themselves. Their general nature is obvious enough, and I do not want to discuss them. I am merely pointing to the fact that, in England, popular imaginative literature is a field that left-wing thought has never begun to enter. *All* fiction from the novels in the mushroom libraries downwards is censored in the interests of the ruling class. And boys' fiction above all, the blood-and-thunder stuff which nearly every boy devours at some time or other, is sodden in the worst illusions of 1910. The fact is only unimportant if one believes that what is read in childhood leaves no impression behind. Lord Camrose and his colleagues evidently believe nothing of the kind, and, after all, Lord Camrose ought to know.

1939.

Charles Dickens

By this time anyone who is a lover of Dickens, and who has read as far as this, will probably be angry with me.

I have been discussing Dickens simply in terms of his "message", and almost ignoring his literary qualities. But every writer, especially every novelist, *has* a "message", whether he admits it or not, and the minutest details of his work are influenced by it. All art is propaganda. Neither Dickens himself nor the majority of Victorian novelists would have thought of denying this. On the other hand, not all propaganda is art. As I said earlier, Dickens is one of those writers who are felt to be worth stealing. He has been stolen by Marxists, by Catholics and, above all, by Conservatives. The question is, What is there to steal? Why does anyone care about Dickens? Why do *I* care about Dickens?

That kind of question is never easy to answer. As a rule, an æsthetic preference is either something inexplicable or it is so corrupted by non-æsthetic motives as to make one wonder whether the whole of literary criticism is not a huge network of humbug. In Dickens's case the complicating factor is his familiarity. He happens to be one of those "great authors" who are ladled down everyone's throat in childhood. At the time this causes rebellion and vomiting, but it may have different after-effects in later life. For instance, nearly everyone feels a sneaking affection for the patriotic poems that he learned by heart as a child, "Ye Mariners of England", the "Charge of the Light Brigade" and so forth. What one enjoys is not so much the poems themselves as the memories they call up. And with Dickens the same forces of association are at work. Probably there are copies of one or two of his books lying about in an actual majority of English homes. Many children begin to know his characters by sight before they can even read, for on the

whole Dickens was lucky in his illustrators. A thing that is
absorbed as early as that does not come up against any critical
judgment. And when one thinks of this, one thinks of all that is
bad and silly in Dickens—the cast-iron "plots", the characters
who don't come off, the *longueurs*, the paragraphs in blank verse,
the awful pages of "pathos". And then the thought arises, when
I say I like Dickens, do I simply mean that I like thinking about
my childhood? Is Dickens merely an institution?

If so, he is an institution that there is no getting away from.
How often one really thinks about any writer, even a writer one
cares for, is a difficult thing to decide; but I should doubt whether
anyone who has actually read Dickens can go a week without
remembering him in one context or another. Whether you
approve of him or not, he is *there*, like the Nelson Column. At
any moment some scene or character, which may come from some
book you cannot even remember the name of, is liable to drop
into your mind. Micawber's letters! Winkle in the witness-box!
Mrs. Gamp! Mrs. Wititterly and Sir Tumley Snuffim! Todgers's!
(George Gissing said that when he passed the Monument it was
never of the Fire of London that he thought, always of Todgers's.)
Mrs. Leo Hunter! Squeers! Silas Wegg and the Decline and
Fall-off of the Russian Empire! Miss Mills and the Desert of
Sahara! Wopsle acting Hamlet! Mrs. Jellyby! Mantalini, Jerry
Cruncher, Barkis, Pumblechook, Tracy Tupman, Skimpole,
Joe Gargery, Pecksniff—and so it goes on and on. It is not so
much a series of books, it is more like a world. And not a purely
comic world either, for part of what one remembers in Dickens
is his Victorian morbidness and necrophilia and the blood-and-
thunder scenes—the death of Sykes, Krook's spontaneous com-
bustion, Fagin in the condemned cell, the women knitting round
the guillotine. To a surprising extent all this has entered even
into the minds of people who do not care about it. A music-hall
comedian can (or at any rate could quite recently) go on the stage
and impersonate Micawber or Mrs. Gamp with a fair certainty
of being understood, although not one in twenty of the audience

had ever read a book of Dickens's right through. Even people who affect to despise him quote him unconsciously.

Dickens is a writer who can be imitated, up to a certain point. In genuinely popular literature—for instance, the Elephant and Castle version of *Sweeney Todd*—he has been plagiarized quite shamelessly. What has been imitated, however, is simply a tradition that Dickens himself took from earlier novelists and developed, the cult of "character", *i.e.* eccentricity. The thing that cannot be imitated is his fertility of invention, which is invention not so much of characters, still less of "situations", as of turns of phrase and concrete details. The outstanding, unmistakable mark of Dickens's writing is the *unnecessary detail*. Here is an example of what I mean. The story given below is not particularly funny, but there is one phrase in it that is as individual as a fingerprint. Mr. Jack Hopkins, at Bob Sawyer's party, is telling the story of the child who swallowed its sister's necklace:

"Next day, child swallowed two beads; the day after that, he treated himself to three, and so on, till in a week's time he had got through the necklace—five-and-twenty beads in all. The sister, who was an industrious girl and seldom treated herself to a bit of finery, cried her eyes out at the loss of the necklace; looked high and low for it; but I needn't say, didn't find it. A few days afterwards, the family were at dinner—baked shoulder of mutton and potatoes under it—the child, who wasn't hungry, was playing about the room, when suddenly there was heard the devil of a noise, like a small hailstorm. 'Don't do that, my boy,' says the father. 'I aint a-doin' nothing,' said the child. 'Well, don't do it again,' said the father. There was a short silence, and then the noise began again, worse than ever. 'If you don't mind what I say, my boy,' said the father, 'you'll find yourself in bed, in something less than a pig's whisper.' He gave the child a shake to make him obedient, and such a rattling ensued as nobody ever heard before. 'Why, dam' me, it's *in* the child,' said the father; 'he's got the croup in the wrong place!' 'No, I haven't, father,' said the child, beginning to cry, 'it's the necklace; I swallowed it, father.' The father caught the child up, and ran with him to the hospital, the beads in the boy's stomach rattling all the way with the jolting; and the people looking up in the air, and down in the cellars, to see where the unusual sound came from. 'He's in the hospital now,' said Jack Hopkins, 'and he makes such a devil of a noise when he walks about, that they're obliged to muffle him in a watchman's coat, for fear he should wake the patients.' "

As a whole, this story might come out of any nineteenth-century comic paper. But the unmistakable Dickens touch, the thing nobody else would have thought of, is the baked shoulder of mutton and potatoes under it. How does this advance the story? The answer is that it doesn't. It is something totally unnecessary, a florid little squiggle on the edge of the page; only, it is by just these squiggles that the special Dickens atmosphere is created. The other thing one would notice here is that Dickens's way of telling a story takes a long time. An interesting example, too long to quote, is Sam Weller's story of the obstinate patient in Chapter XLIV of *The Pickwick Papers*. As it happens, we have a standard of comparison here, because Dickens is plagiarizing, consciously or unconsciously. The story is also told by some ancient Greek writer. I cannot now find the passage, but I read it years ago as a boy at school, and it runs more or less like this:

"A certain Thracian, renowned for his obstinacy, was warned by his physician that if he drank a flagon of wine it would kill him. The Thracian thereupon drank the flagon of wine and immediately jumped off the house-top and perished. 'For,' said he, 'in this way I shall prove that the wine did not kill me.' "

As the Greek tells it, that is the whole story—about six lines. As Sam Weller tells it, it takes round about a thousand words. Long before getting to the point we have been told all about the patient's clothes, his meals, his manners, even the newspapers he reads, and about the peculiar construction of the doctor's carriage, which conceals the fact that the coachman's trousers do not match his coat. Then there is the dialogue between the doctor and the patient. " 'Crumpets is wholesome, sir,' said the patient. 'Crumpets is *not* wholesome, sir,' says the doctor, wery fierce," etc., etc. In the end the original story has been buried under the details. And in all of Dickens's most characteristic passages it is the same. His imagination overwhelms everything, like a kind of weed. Squeers stands up to address his boys, and immediately we are hearing about Bolder's father who was two pounds ten short, and Mobbs's stepmother who took to her bed on hearing that Mobbs wouldn't eat fat and hoped Mr. Squeers would flog him into a happier state of mind. Mrs. Leo Hunter writes a poem, "Expiring Frog"; two full stanzas are given. Boffin takes a fancy to pose as a miser, and instantly we are down among the squalid biographies of eighteenth-century misers, with names like Vulture Hopkins and the Rev. Blewberry Jones, and chapter headings like "The Story of the Mutton Pies" and "The Treasures of a Dunghill". Mrs. Harris, who does not even exist, has more detail piled on to her than any three characters in an ordinary novel. Merely in the middle of a sentence we learn, for instance, that her infant nephew has been seen in a bottle at Greenwich Fair, along with the pink-eyed lady, the Prussian dwarf and the living skeleton. Joe Gargery describes how the robbers broke into the house of Pumblechook, the corn and seed merchant—"and they took his till, and they took his cashbox, and they drinked his wine, and they partook of his wittles, and they slapped his face, and they pulled his nose, and they tied him up to his bedpost, and they give him a dozen, and they stuffed his mouth full of flowering annuals to perwent his crying out". Once again the unmistakable Dickens touch, the flowering annuals; but any other novelist would only have mentioned about half of these outrages. Everything is piled up and up, detail on detail, embroidery on embroidery. It is futile to object that this kind of thing is rococo—one might as well make the same objection to a wedding-cake. Either you like it or you do not like it. Other nineteenth-century writers, Surtees, Barham, Thackeray, even Marryat, have something of Dickens's profuse, overflowing quality, but none of them on anything like the same scale. The appeal of all these writers now depends partly on period-flavour, and though Marryat is still officially a "boy's writer" and Surtees has a sort of legendary fame among hunting men, it is probable that they are read mostly by bookish people.

Significantly, Dickens's most successful books (not his *best* books) are *The Pickwick Papers*, which is not a novel, and *Hard Times* and *A Tale of Two Cities*, which are not funny. As a novelist his natural fertility greatly hampers him, because the burlesque which he is never able to resist, is constantly breaking into what ought to be serious situations. There is a good example of this in the opening chapter of *Great Expectations*. The escaped convict, Magwitch, has just captured the six-year-old Pip in the churchyard. The scene starts terrifyingly enough, from Pip's point of view. The convict, smothered in mud and with his chain trailing from his leg, suddenly starts up among the tombs, grabs the child, turns him upside down and robs his pockets. Then he begins terrorizing him into bringing food and a file:

"He held me by the arms, in an upright position on the top of the stone, and went on in these fearful terms:

" 'You bring me, to-morrow morning early, that file and them wittles. You bring the lot to me, at that old Battery over yonder. You do it, and you never dare to say a word or dare to make a sign concerning your having seen such a person as me, or any person sumever, and you shall be let to live. You fail, or you go from my words in any partickler, no matter how small it is, and your heart and liver shall be tore out, roasted and ate. Now, I ain't alone, as you may think I am. There's a young man hid with me, in comparison with which young man I am a Angel. That young man hears the words I speak. That young man has a secret pecooliar to himself, of getting at a boy, and at his heart, and at his liver. It is in wain for a boy to attempt to hide himself from that young man. A boy may lock his door, may be warm in bed, may tuck himself up, may draw the clothes over his head, may think himself comfortable and safe, but that young man will softly creep his way to him and tear him open. I am a-keeping that young man from harming of you at the present moment, with great difficulty. I find it wery hard to hold that young man off of your inside. Now, what do you say?' "

Here Dickens has simply yielded to temptation. To begin with, no starving and hunted man would speak in the least like that. Moreover, although the speech shows a remarkable knowledge of the way in which a child's mind works, its actual words are quite out of tune with what is to follow. It turns Magwitch into a sort of pantomime wicked uncle, or, if one sees him through the child's eyes, into an appalling monster. Later in the book he is to be represented as neither, and his exaggerated gratitude, on which the plot turns, is to be incredible because of just this speech. As usual, Dickens's imagination has over-whelmed him. The picturesque details were too good to be left out. Even with characters who are more of a piece than Magwitch he is liable to be tripped up by some seductive phrase. Mr. Murdstone, for instance, is in the habit of ending David Copper-field's lessons every morning with a dreadful sum in arithmetic. "If I go into a cheesemonger's shop, and buy four thousand double-Gloucester cheeses at fourpence halfpenny each, present payment," it always begins. Once again the typical Dickens detail, the double-Gloucester cheeses. But it is far too human a touch for Murdstone; he would have made it five thousand cashboxes. Every time this note is struck, the unity of the novel suffers. Not that it matters very much, because Dickens is obviously a writer whose parts are greater than his wholes. He is all fragments, all details—rotten architecture, but wonderful gargoyles—and never better than when he is building up some character who will later on be forced to act inconsistently.

Of course it is not usual to urge against Dickens that he makes his characters behave inconsistently. Generally he is accused of doing just the opposite. His characters are supposed to be mere "types", each crudely representing some single trait and fitted with a kind of label by which you recognize him. Dickens is "only a caricaturist"—that is the usual accusation, and it does him both more and less than justice. To begin with, he did not think of himself as a caricaturist, and was constantly setting into action characters who ought to have been purely static. Squeers,

Micawber, Miss Mowcher,[1] Wegg, Skimpole, Pecksniff and many others are finally involved in "plots" where they are out of place and where they behave quite incredibly. They start off as magic-lantern slides and they end by getting mixed up in a third-rate movie. Sometimes one can put one's finger on a single sentence in which the original illusion is destroyed. There is such a sentence in *David Copperfield*. After the famous dinner-party (the one where the leg of mutton was underdone), David is showing his guests out. He stops Traddles at the top of the stairs:

> " 'Traddles,' said I, 'Mr. Micawber don't mean any harm, poor fellow: but if I were you I wouldn't lend him anything.'
> " 'My dear Copperfield,' returned Traddles smiling, 'I haven't got anything to lend.'
> " 'You have got a name, you know,' I said."

At the place where one reads it this remark jars a little though something of the kind was inevitable sooner or later. The story is a fairly realistic one, and David is growing up; ultimately he is bound to see Mr. Micawber for what he is, a cadging scoundrel. Afterwards, of course, Dickens's sentimentality overcomes him and Micawber is made to turn over a new leaf. But from then on, the original Micawber is never quite recaptured, in spite of desperate efforts. As a rule, the "plot" in which Dickens's characters get entangled is not particularly credible, but at least it makes some pretence at reality, whereas the world to which they belong is a never-never land, a kind of eternity. But just here one sees that "only a caricaturist" is not really a condemnation. The fact that Dickens is always thought of as a caricaturist, although he was constantly trying to be something else, is perhaps the surest mark of his genius. The monstrosities that he created are still remembered as monstrosities, in spite of getting mixed up in would-be probable melodramas. Their

[1] Dickens turned Miss Mowcher into a sort of heroine because the real woman whom he had caricatured had read the earlier chapters and was bitterly hurt. He had previously meant her to play a villainous part. But *any* action by such a character would seem incongruous.

first impact is so vivid that nothing that comes afterwards effaces it. As with the people one knew in childhood, one seems always to remember them in one particular attitude, doing one particular thing. Mrs. Squeers is always ladling out brimstone and treacle, Mrs. Gummidge is always weeping, Mrs. Gargery is always banging her husband's head against the wall, Mrs. Jellyby is always scribbling tracts while her children fall into the area—and there they all are, fixed up for ever like little twinkling miniatures painted on snuffbox lids, completely fantastic and incredible, and yet somehow more solid and infinitely more memorable than the efforts of serious novelists. Even by the standards of his time Dickens was an exceptionally artificial writer. As Ruskin said, he "chose to work in a circle of stage fire". His characters are even more distorted and simplified than Smollett's. But there are no rules in novel-writing, and for any work of art there is only one test worth bothering about—survival. By this test Dickens's characters have succeeded, even if the people who remember them hardly think of them as human beings. They are monsters, but at any rate they *exist*.

But all the same there is a disadvantage in writing about monsters. It amounts to this, that it is only certain moods that Dickens can speak to. There are large areas of the human mind that he never touches. There is no poetic feeling anywhere in his books, and no genuine tragedy, and even sexual love is almost outside his scope. Actually his books are not so sexless as they are sometimes declared to be, and considering the time in which he was writing, he is reasonably frank. But there is not a trace in him of the feeling that one finds in *Manon Lescaut*, *Salammbô*, *Carmen*, *Wuthering Heights*. According to Aldous Huxley, D. H. Lawrence once said that Balzac was "a gigantic dwarf", and in a sense the same is true of Dickens. There are whole worlds which he either knows nothing about or does not wish to mention. Except in a rather roundabout way, one cannot *learn* very much from Dickens. And to say this is to think almost immediately of the great Russian novelists of the nineteenth

century. Why is it that Tolstoy's grasp seems to be so much
larger than Dickens's—why is it that he seems able to tell you
so much more *about yourself*? It is not that he is more gifted, or
even, in the last analysis, more intelligent. It is because he is
writing about people who are growing. His characters are
struggling to make their souls, whereas Dickens's are already
finished and perfect. In my own mind Dickens's people are
present far more often and far more vividly than Tolstoy's, but
always in a single unchangeable attitude, like pictures or pieces
of furniture. You cannot hold an imaginary conversation with a
Dickens character as you can with, say, Peter Bezoukhov. And
this is not merely because of Tolstoy's greater seriousness, for
there are also comic characters that you can imagine yourself
talking to—Bloom, for instance, or Pécuchet, or even Wells's
Mr. Polly. It is because Dickens's characters have no mental life.
They say perfectly the thing that they have to say, but they
cannot be conceived as talking about anything else. They never
learn, never speculate. Perhaps the most meditative of his
characters is Paul Dombey, and his thoughts are mush. Does
this mean that Tolstoy's novels are "better" than Dickens's?
The truth is that it is absurd to make such comparisons in terms
of "better" and "worse". If I were forced to compare Tolstoy
with Dickens, I should say that Tolstoy's appeal will probably
be wider in the long run, because Dickens is scarcely intelligible
outside the English-speaking culture; on the other hand, Dickens
is able to reach simple people, which Tolstoy is not. Tolstoy's
characters can cross a frontier, Dickens can be portrayed on a
cigarette-card. But one is no more obliged to choose between
them than between a sausage and a rose. Their purposes barely
intersect.

If Dickens had been *merely* a comic writer, the chances are
that no one would now remember his name. Or at best a few of
his books would survive in rather the same way as books like
Frank Fairleigh, *Mr. Verdant Green* and *Mrs. Caudle's Curtain*

Lectures, as a sort of hangover of the Victorian atmosphere, a pleasant little whiff of oysters and brown stout. Who has not felt sometimes that it was "a pity" that Dickens ever deserted the vein of *Pickwick* for things like *Little Dorrit* and *Hard Times*? What people always demand of a popular novelist is that he shall write the same book over and over again, forgetting that a man who would write the same book twice could not even write it once. Any writer who is not utterly lifeless moves upon a kind of parabola, and the downward curve is implied in the upper one. Joyce has to start with the frigid competence of *Dubliners* and end with the dream-language of *Finnegan's Wake,* but *Ulysses* and *Portrait of an Artist* are part of the trajectory. The thing that drove Dickens forward into a form of art for which he was not really suited, and at the same time caused us to remember him, was simply the fact that he was a moralist, the consciousness of "having something to say". He is always preaching a sermon, and that is the final secret of his inventiveness. For you can only create if you can *care.* Types like Squeers and Micawber could not have been produced by a hack writer looking for something to be funny about. A joke worth laughing at always has an idea behind it, and usually a subversive idea. Dickens is able to go on being funny because he is in revolt against authority, and authority is always there to be laughed at. There is always room for one more custard pie.

His radicalism is of the vaguest kind, and yet one always knows that it is there. That is the difference between being a moralist and a politician. He has no constructive suggestions, not even a clear grasp of the nature of the society he is attacking, only an emotional perception that something is wrong. All he can finally say is, "Behave decently", which, as I suggested earlier, is not necessarily so shallow as it sounds. Most revolutionaries are potential Tories, because they imagine that everything can be put right by altering the *shape* of society; once that change is effected, as it sometimes is, they see no need for any other. Dickens has not this kind of mental coarseness. The vagueness of his discontent is the mark of its permanence. What he is out against is not this or that institution, but, as Chesterton put it, "an expression on the human face". Roughly speaking, his morality is the Christian morality, but in spite of his Anglican upbringing he was essentially a Bible-Christian, as he took care to make plain when writing his will. In any case he cannot properly be described as a religious man. He "believed", undoubtedly, but religion in the devotional sense does not seem to have entered much into his thoughts.[1] Where he is Christian is in his quasi-instinctive siding with the oppressed against the oppressors. As a matter of course he is on the side of the underdog, always and everywhere. To carry this to its logical conclusion one has got to change sides when the underdog becomes an upperdog, and in fact Dickens does tend to do so. He loathes the Catholic Church, for instance, but as soon as the Catholics are persecuted (*Barnaby Rudge*) he is on their side. He loathes the aristocratic class even more, but as soon as they are really overthrown (the revolutionary chapters in *A Tale of Two Cities*) his sympathies swing round. Whenever he departs from this emotional attitude he goes astray. A well-known example is at the ending of *David Copperfield*, in which everyone who reads it feels that something has gone wrong. What is wrong is that the closing chapters are pervaded, faintly but not noticeably, by the cult of success. It is the gospel according to Smiles, instead of the gospel according to Dickens. The attractive, out-at-elbow characters are got rid of, Micawber makes a fortune, Heep gets into prison—both of these events are flagrantly impossible—

---

[1] From a letter to his youngest son (in 1868): "You will remember that you have never at home been harassed about religious observances, or mere formalities. I have always been anxious not to weary my children with such things, before they are old enough to form opinions respecting them. You will therefore understand the better that I now most solemnly impress upon you the truth and beauty of the Christian Religion, as it came from Christ Himself, and the impossibility of your going far wrong if you humbly but heartily respect it. . . . Never abandon the wholesome practice of saying your own private prayers, night and morning. I have never abandoned it myself, and I know the comfort of it."

d even Dora is killed off to make way for Agnes. If you like,
u can read Dora as Dickens's wife and Agnes as his sister-in-
v, but the essential point is that Dickens has "turned respect-
le" and done violence to his own nature. Perhaps that is why
;nes is the most disagreeable of his heroines, the real legless
gel of Victorian romance, almost as bad as Thackeray's Laura.
No grown-up person can read Dickens without feeling his
nitations, and yet there does remain his native generosity of
ind, which acts as a kind of anchor and nearly always keeps
m where he belongs. It is probably the central secret of his
pularity. A good-tempered antinomianism rather of Dickens's
pe is one of the marks of Western popular culture. One sees it
folk-stories and comic songs, in dream-figures like Mickey
ouse and Pop-eye the Sailor (both of them variants of Jack
e Giant-killer), in the history of working-class Socialism, in
e popular protests (always ineffective but not always a sham)
ainst imperialism, in the impulse that makes a jury award
cessive damages when a rich man's car runs over a poor
an; it is the feeling that one is always on the side of the
derdog, on the side of the weak against the strong. In one
nse it is a feeling that is fifty years out of date. The common
an is still living in the mental world of Dickens, but nearly
ery modern intellectual has gone over to some or other form
totalitarianism. From the Marxist or Fascist point of view,
arly all that Dickens stands for can be written off as "bourgeois
orality". But in moral outlook no one could be more "bourgeois"
an the English working classes. The ordinary people in the
estern countries have never entered, mentally, into the world
"realism" and power-politics. They may do so before long, in
hich case Dickens will be as out of date as the cab-horse. But in
s own age and ours he has been popular chiefly because he was
le to express in a comic, simplified and therefore memorable
rm the native decency of the common man. And it is im-
rtant that from this point of view people of very different
pes can be described as "common". In a country like England,

in spite of its class-structure, there does exist a certain cultu
unity. All through the Christian ages, and especially since t
French Revolution, the Western world has been haunted by t
idea of freedom and equality; it is only an *idea*, but it h
penetrated to all ranks of society. The most atrocious injustic
cruelties, lies, snobberies exist everywhere, but there are r
many people who can regard these things with the same i
difference as, say, a Roman slave-owner. Even the milliona
suffers from a vague sense of guilt, like a dog eating a stolen l
of mutton. Nearly everyone, whatever his actual conduct m
be, responds emotionally to the idea of human brotherho
Dickens voiced a code which was and on the whole still is believ
in, even by people who violate it. It is difficult otherwise
explain why he could be both read by working people (a thi
that has happened to no other novelist of his stature) and buri
in Westminster Abbey.

When one reads any strongly individual piece of writing, o
has the impression of seeing a face somewhere behind the pag
It is not necessarily the actual face of the writer. I feel th
very strongly with Swift, with Defoe, with Fielding, Stendh
Thackeray, Flaubert, though in several cases I do not kno
what these people looked like and do not want to know. Wh
one sees is the face that the writer *ought* to have. Well, in t
case of Dickens I see a face that is not quite the face of Dickens
photographs, though it resembles it. It is the face of a man
about forty, with a small beard and a high colour. He is laughin
with a touch of anger in his laughter, but no triumph, r
malignity. It is the face of a man who is always fighting again
something, but who fights in the open and is not frightened, th
face of a man who is *generously angry*—in other words, of
nineteenth-century liberal, a free intelligence, a type hated wi
equal hatred by all the smelly little orthodoxies which are no
contending for our souls.

1939.

The Sporting Spirit

Now that the brief visit of the Dynamo football team [1] has come
an end, it is possible to say publicly what many thinking people
ere saying privately before the Dynamos ever arrived. That is,
at sport is an unfailing cause of ill-will, and that if such a visit
this had any effect at all on Anglo-Soviet relations, it could
ly be to make them slightly worse than before.

Even the newspapers have been unable to conceal the fact
at at least two of the four matches played led to much bad
eling. At the Arsenal match, I am told by someone who was
ere, a British and a Russian player came to blows and the
owd booed the referee. The Glasgow match, someone else
forms me, was simply a free-for-all from the start. And then
ere was the controversy, typical of our nationalistic age, about
e composition of the Arsenal team. Was it really an all-England
am, as claimed by the Russians, or merely a league team, as
aimed by the British? And did the Dynamos end their tour
oruptly in order to avoid playing an all-England team? As
ual, everyone answers these questions according to his
olitical predilections. No doubt the controversy will continue
 echo for years in the footnotes of history books. Meanwhile
 e result of the Dynamos' tour, in so far as it has had
 y result, will have been to create fresh animosity on both
des.

And how could it be otherwise? I am always amazed when I
ear people saying that sport creates goodwill between the
tions, and that if only the common peoples of the world could
eet one another at football or cricket, they would have no
clination to meet on the battlefield. Even if one didn't know
om concrete examples (the 1936 Olympic Games, for instan

[1] The Moscow Dynamos, a Russian football team, toured Britain in
e autumn of 1945 playing against leading clubs.

that internatioanal sporting contests lead to orgies of hatred, o
could deduce it from general principles.

Nearly all the sports practised nowadays are competitive. Y
play to win, and the game has little meaning unless you do yo
utmost to win. On the village green, where you pick up sid
and no feeling of local patriotism is involved, it is possible
play simply for the fun and exercise: but as soon as the questi
of prestige arises, as soon as you feel that you and some larg
unit will be disgraced if you lose, the most savage combati
instincts are aroused. Anyone who has played even in a scho
football match knows this. At the international level sport
frankly mimic warfare. But the significant thing is not th
behaviour of the players but the attitude of the spectators: an
behind the spectators, of the nations who work themselves in
furies over these absurd contests, and seriously believe—at an
rate for short periods—that running, jumping and kicking a ba
are tests of national virtue.

Even a leisurely game like cricket, demanding grace rath
than strength, can cause much ill-will, as we saw in the contr
versy over body-line bowling and over the rough tactics of th
Australian team that visited England in 1921. Football, a gam
in which everyone gets hurt and every nation has its own sty
of play which seems unfair to foreigners, is far worse. Worst
all is boxing. One of the most horrible sights in the world is
fight between white and coloured boxers before a mixed audienc
But a boxing audience is always disgusting, and the behaviour
the women, in particular, is such that the Army, I believe, do
not allow them to attend its contests. At any rate, two or thre
years ago, when Home Guards and regular troops were holding
boxing tournament, I was placed on guard at the door of th
hall, with orders to keep the women out.

In England, the obsession with sport is bad enough, but eve
fiercer passions are aroused in young countries where gam
playing and nationalism are both recent developments. I
countries like India or Burma, it is necessary at football matche

to have strong cordons of police to keep the crowd from invading the field. In Burma, I have seen the supporters of one side break through the police and disable the goalkeeper of the opposing side at a critical moment. The first big football match that was played in Spain about fifteen years ago, led to an uncontrollable riot. As soon as strong feelings of rivalry are aroused, the notion of playing the game according to the rules always vanishes. People want to see one side on top and the other side humiliated and they forget that victory gained through cheating or through the intervention of the crowd is meaningless. Even when the spectators don't intervene physically they try to influence the game by cheering their own side and "rattling" opposing players with boos and insults. Serious sport has nothing to do with fair play. It is bound up with hatred, jealousy, boastfulness, disregard of all rules and sadistic pleasure in witnessing violence: in other words it is war minus the shooting.

Instead of blah-blahing about the clean, healthy rivalry of the football field and the great part played by the Olympic Games in bringing the nations together, it is more useful to inquire how and why this modern cult of sport arose. Most of the games we now play are of ancient origin, but sport does not seem to have been taken very seriously between Roman times and the nineteenth century. Even in the English public schools the games cult did not start till the later part of the last century. Dr. Arnold, generally regarded as the founder of the modern public school, looked on games as simply a waste of time. Then, chiefly in England and the United States, games were built up into a heavily-financed activity, capable of attracting vast crowds and rousing savage passions, and the infection spread from country to country. It is the most violently combative sports, football and boxing, that have spread the widest. There cannot be much doubt that the whole thing is bound up with the rise of nationalism—that is, with the lunatic modern habit of identifying oneself with large power units and seeing everything in terms of competitive prestige. Also, organized games are more likely to flourish in urban communities where the average human being lives a sedentary or at least a confined life, and does not get much opportunity for creative labour. In a rustic community a boy or young man works off a good deal of his surplus energy by walking, swimming, snowballing, climbing trees, riding horses, and by various sports involving cruelty to animals, such as fishing, cock-fighting and ferreting for rats. In a big town one must indulge in group activities if one wants an outlet for one's physical strength or for one's sadistic impulses. Games are taken seriously in London and New York, and they were taken seriously in Rome and Byzantium: in the Middle Ages they were played, and probably played with much physical brutality, but they were not mixed up with politics nor a cause of group hatreds.

If you wanted to add to the vast fund of ill-will existing in the world at this moment, you could hardly do it better than by a series of football matches between Jews and Arabs, Germans and Czechs, Indians and British, Russians and Poles, and Italians and Yugoslavs, each match to be watched by a mixed audience of 100,000 spectators. I do not, of course, suggest that sport is one of the main causes of international rivalry; big-scale sport is itself, I think, merely another effect of the causes that have produced nationalism. Still, you do make things worse by sending forth a team of eleven men, labelled as national champions, to do battle against some rival team, and allowing it to be felt on all sides that whichever nation is defeated will "lose face".

I hope, therefore, that we shan't follow up the visit of the Dynamos by sending a British team to the U.S.S.R. If we must do so, then let us send a second-rate team which is sure to be beaten and cannot be claimed to represent Britain as a whole. There are quite enough real causes of trouble already, and we need not add to them by encouraging young men to kick each other on the shins amid the roars of infuriated spectators.

1945.

The Re-writing of History

With the deep, unconscious sigh which not even the nearness of the telescreen could prevent him from uttering when his day's work started, Winston pulled the speakwrite towards him, blew the dust from its mouthpiece and put on his spectacles. Then he unrolled and clipped together four small cylinders of paper which had already flopped out of the pneumatic tube on the right-hand side of his desk.

In the walls of the cubicle there were three orifices. To the right of the speakwrite, a small pneumatic tube for written messages; to the left, a larger one for newspapers; and in the side wall, within easy reach of Winston's arm, a large oblong slit protected by a wire grating. This last was for the disposal of waste paper. Similar slits existed in thousands or tens of thousands throughout the building, not only in every room but at short intervals in every corridor. For some reason they were nicknamed memory holes. When one knew that any document was due for destruction, or even when one saw a scrap of waste paper lying about, it was an automatic action to lift the flap of the nearest memory hole and drop it in, whereupon it would be whirled away on a current of warm air to the enormous furnaces which were hidden somewhere in the recesses of the building.

Winston examined the four slips of paper which he had unrolled. Each contained a message of only one or two lines, in the abbreviated jargon—not actually Newspeak, but consisting largely of Newspeak words—which was used in the Ministry for internal purposes. They ran:

times 17.3.84 bb speech malreported africa rectify

times 19.12.83 forecasts 3 yp 4th quarter 83 misprints verify current issue times 14.2.84 miniplenty malquoted chocolate rectify

times 3.12.83 reporting bb dayorder doubleplusungood refs unpersons rewrite fullwise upsub antefiling

With a faint feeling of satisfaction Winston laid the fourth message aside. It was an intricate and responsible job and had better be dealt with last. The other three were routine matters, though the second one would probably mean some tedious wading through lists of figures.

Winston dialled "back numbers" on the telescreen and called for the appropriate issues of the *Times*, which slid out of the pneumatic tube after only a few minutes' delay. The messages he had received referred to articles or news-items which for one reason or another it was thought necessary to alter, or, as the official phrase had it, to rectify. For example, it appeared from the *Times* of the seventeenth of March that Big Brother, in his speech of the previous day, had predicted that the South Indian front would remain quiet but that a Eurasian offensive would shortly be launched in North Africa. As it happened the Eurasian Higher Command had launched its offensive in South India and left North Africa alone. It was therefore necessary to rewrite a paragraph of Big Brother's speech, in such a way as to make him predict the thing that had actually happened. Or again, the *Times* of the nineteenth of December had published the official forecasts of the output of various classes of consumption goods in the fourth quarter of 1983, which was also the sixth quarter of the Ninth Three-Year Plan. To-day's issue contained a statement of the actual output, from which it appeared that the forecasts were in every instance grossly wrong. Winston's job was to rectify the original figures by making them agree with the later ones. As for the third message, it referred to a very simple error which could be set right in a couple of minutes. As short a time ago as February, the Ministry of Plenty had issued a promise (a "categorical pledge" were the official words) that there would be no reduction of the chocolate ration during 1984. Actually, as Winston was aware, the chocolate ration was to be reduced from thirty grammes to twenty at the end of the present week. All that was needed was to substitute for the original promise a warning that it would probably be necessary to reduce the ration at some time in April.

As soon as Winston had dealt with each of the messages, he clipped his speakwritten corrections to the appropriate copy of the *Times* and pushed them into the pneumatic tube. Then, with a movement which was as nearly as possible unconscious, he crumpled up the original message and any notes that he himself had made, and dropped them into the memory hole to be devoured by the flames.

What happened in the unseen labyrinth to which the pneumatic tubes led, he did not know in detail, but he did know in general terms. As soon as all the corrections which happened to be necessary in any particular number of the *Times* had been assembled and collated, that number would be reprinted, the original copy destroyed, and the corrected copy placed on the files in its stead. This process of continuous alteration was applied not only to newspapers, but to books, periodicals, pamphlets, posters, leaflets, films, sound-tracks, cartoons, photographs—to every kind of literature or documentation which might conceivably hold any political or ideological significance. Day by day and almost minute by minute the past was brought up to date. In this way every prediction made by the Party could be shown by documentary evidence to have been correct; nor was any item of news, or any expression of opinion, which conflicted with the needs of the moment, ever allowed to remain on record. All history was a palimpsest, scraped clean and re-inscribed exactly as often as was necessary. In no case would it have been possible, once the deed was done, to prove that any falsification had taken place. The largest section of the Records Department, far larger than the one in which Winston worked, consisted simply of persons whose duty it was to track down and collect all copies of books, newspapers and other documents which had been superseded and were due for destruction. A number of the *Times* which might, because of changes in political alignment, or mistaken prophecies uttered by Big Brother, have been re-written a dozen times still stood on the files bearing its original date, and no other copy existed to contradict it. Books, also, were recalled and rewritten again and again, and were invariably reissued without any admission that any alteration had been made. Even the written instructions which Winston received, and which he invariably got rid of as soon as he had dealt with them, never stated or implied that an act of forgery was to be committed: always the reference was to slips, errors, misprints or misquotations which it was necessary to put right in the interests of accuracy.

But actually, he thought as he re-adjusted the Ministry of Plenty's figures, it was not even forgery. It was merely the substitution of one piece of nonsense for another. Most of the material that you were dealing with had no connexion with anything in the real world, not even the kind of connexion that is contained in a direct lie. Statistics were just as much a fantasy in their original version as in their rectified version. A great deal of the time you were expected to make them up out of your head. For example, the Ministry of Plenty's forecast had estimated the output of boots for the quarter at a hundred and forty-five million pairs. The actual output was given as sixty-two millions. Winston, however, in re-writing the forecast, marked the figure down to fifty-seven millions, so as to allow for the usual claim that the quota had been overfulfilled. In any case, sixty-two millions was no nearer the truth than fifty-seven millions, or than a hundred and forty-five millions. Very likely no boots had been produced at all. Likelier still, nobody knew how many had been produced, much less cared. All one knew was that every quarter astronomical numbers of boots were produced on paper, while perhaps half the population of Oceania went barefoot. And so it was with every class of recorded fact, great or small. Everything faded away into a shadow-world in which, finally, even the date of the year had become uncertain.

Winston glanced across the hall. In the corresponding cubicle on the other side a small, precise-looking, dark-chinned man named Tillotson was working steadily away, with a folded newspaper on his knee and his mouth very close to the mouthpiece of the speakwrite. He had the air of trying to keep what he was saying a secret between himself and the telescreen. He looked up, and his spectacles darted a hostile flash in Winston's direction.

Winston hardly knew Tillotson, and had no idea what work he was employed on. People in the Records Department did not readily talk about their jobs. In the long, windowless hall, with its double row of cubicles and its endless rustle of papers and hum of voices murmuring into speakwrites, there were quite a dozen people whom Winston did not even know by name, though he daily saw them hurrying to and fro in the corridors or gesticulating in the Two Minutes Hate. He knew that in the cubicle next to him the little woman with sandy hair toiled day in and day out, simply at tracking down and deleting from the press the names of people who had been vapourized and were therefore considered never to have existed. There was a certain fitness in this, since her own husband had been vapourized a couple of years earlier. And a few cubicles away a mild, ineffectual, dreamy creature named Ampleforth, with very hairy ears and a surprising talent for juggling with rhymes and metres, was engaged in producing garbled versions—definitive texts, they were called—of poems which had become ideologically offensive but which for one reason or another were to be retained in the anthologies. And this hall, with its fifty workers or thereabouts, was only one sub-section, a single cell, as it were, in the huge complexity of the Records Department. Beyond, above, below, were other swarms of workers engaged in an unimaginable multitude of jobs. There were the huge printing shops with their sub-editors, their typography experts and their elaborately equipped studios for the faking of photographs. There was the tele-programmes section with its engineers, its producers and its teams of actors specially chosen for their skill in imitating voices. There were the armies of reference clerks whose job was simply to draw up lists of books and periodicals which were due for recall. There were the vast repositories where the corrected documents were stored, and the hidden furnaces where the original copies were destroyed. And somewhere or other, quite anonymous, there were the directing brains who co-ordinated the whole effort and laid down the lines of policy which made it necessary that this fragment of the past should be preserved, that one falsified, and the other rubbed out of existence.

And the Records Department, after all, was itself only a single branch of the Ministry of Truth, whose primary job was not to reconstruct the past but to supply the citizens of Oceania with newspapers, films, textbooks, telescreen programmes, plays, novels—with every conceivable kind of information, instruction or entertainment, from a statue to a slogan, from a lyric poem to a biological treatise, and from a child's spelling book to a New-speak dictionary. And the Ministry had not only to supply the multifarious needs of the Party, but also to repeat the whole operation at a lower level for the benefit of the proletariat. There was a whole chain of separate departments dealing with prole-tarian literature, music, drama and entertainment generally. Here were produced rubbishy newspapers containing almost nothing except sport, crime and astrology, sensational five-cent novelettes, films oozing with sex, and sentimental songs which were composed entirely by mechanical means on a special kind of kaleidoscope known as a versificator. There was even a whole sub-section—*Pornosec*, it was called in Newspeak—engaged in producing the lowest kind of pornography, which was sent out in sealed packets and which no Party member, other than those who worked on it, was permitted to look at.

Three messages had slid out of the pneumatic tube while Winston was working; but they were simple matters, and he had disposed of them before the Two Minutes Hate interrupted him. When the Hate was over he returned to his cubicle, took the Newspeak dictionary from the shelf, pushed the speakwrite to one side, cleaned his spectacles and settled down to his main job of the morning.

Winston's greatest pleasure in life was in his work. Most of it was a tedious routine, but included in it there were also jobs so difficult and intricate that you could lose yourself in them as in the depths of a mathematical problem—delicate pieces of forgery in which you had nothing to guide you except your knowledge of the principles of Ingsoc and your estimate of what the Party wanted you to say. Winston was good at this kind of thing. On occasion he had even been entrusted with the rectification of the *Times* leading articles, which were written entirely in New-speak. He unrolled the message that he had set aside earlier. It ran:

times 3.12.83 reporting bb dayorder doubleplusungood refs unpersons rewrite fullwise upsub antefiling

In Oldspeak (or standard English) this might be rendered:

The reporting of Big Brother's Order for the Day in the *Times* of December 3rd 1983 is extremely unsatisfactory and makes references to non-existent persons. Rewrite it in full and submit your draft to higher authority before filing.

Winston read through the offending article. Big Brother's Order for the Day, it seemed, had been chiefly devoted to praising the work of an organization known as FFCC, which supplied cigarettes and other comforts to the sailors in the Floating Fortresses. A certain Comrade Withers, a prominent member of the Inner Party, had been singled out for special mention and awarded a decoration, the Order of Conspicuous Merit, Second Class.

Three months later FFCC had suddenly been dissolved with no reasons given. One could assume that Withers and his associates were now in disgrace, but there had been no report of the matter in the press or on the telescreen. That was to be expected, since it was unusual for political offenders to be put on trial or even publicly denounced. The great purges involving thousands of people, with public trials of traitors and thought-criminals who made abject confession of their crimes and were afterwards executed, were special show-pieces not occurring oftener than once in a couple of years. More commonly, people who had incurred the displeasure of the Party simply disappeared and were never heard of again. One never had the smallest clue as to what had happened to them. In some cases they might not even be dead. Perhaps thirty people personally known to Winston, not counting his parents, had disappeared at one time or another.

Winston stroked his nose gently with a paper-clip. In the cubicle across the way Comrade Tillotson was still crouching secretively over his speakwrite. He raised his head for a moment: again the hostile spectacle-flash. Winston wondered whether Comrade Tillotson was engaged on the same job as himself. It was perfectly possible. So tricky a piece of work would never be entrusted to a single person: on the other hand, to turn it over to a committee would be to admit openly that an act of fabrication was taking place. Very likely as many as a dozen people were now working away on rival versions of what Big Brother had actually said. And presently some master brain in the Inner Party would select this version or that, would re-edit it and set in motion the complex processes of cross-referencing that would be required, and then the chosen lie would pass into the permanent records and become truth.

Winston did not know why Withers had been disgraced. Perhaps it was for corruption or incompetence. Perhaps Big Brother was merely getting rid of a too-popular subordinate. Perhaps Withers or someone close to him had been suspected of heretical tendencies. Or perhaps—what was likeliest of all—

the thing had simply happened because purges and vapourizations were a necessary part of the mechanics of government. The only real clue lay in the words "refs unpersons", which indicated that Withers was already dead. You could not invariably assume this to be the case when people were arrested. Sometimes they were released and allowed to remain at liberty for as much as a year or two years before being executed. Very occasionally some person whom you had believed dead long since would make a ghostly reappearance at some public trial where he would implicate hundreds of others by his testimony before vanishing, this time for ever. Withers, however, was already an *unperson*. He did not exist: he had never existed. Winston decided that it would not be enough simply to reverse the tendency of Big Brother's speech. It was better to make it deal with something totally unconnected with its original subject.

He might turn the speech into the usual denunciation of traitors and thought-criminals, but that was a little too obvious; while to invent a victory at the front, or some triumph of over-production in the Ninth Three-Year Plan, might complicate the records too much. What was needed was a piece of pure fantasy. Suddenly there sprang into his mind, ready made as it were, the image of a certain Comrade Ogilvy, who had recently died in battle, in heroic circumstances. There were occasions when Big Brother devoted his Order for the Day to commemorating some humble, rank-and-file Party member whose life and death he held up as an example worthy to be followed. To-day he should commemorate Comrade Ogilvy. It was true that there was no such person as Comrade Ogilvy, but a few lines of print and a couple of faked photographs would soon bring him into existence.

Winston thought for a moment, then pulled the speakwrite towards him and began dictating in Big Brother's familiar style: a style at once military and pedantic, and, because of a trick of asking questions and then promptly answering them ("What lessons do we learn from this fact, comrades? The lesson—

which is also one of the fundamental principles of Ingsoc—that," etc., etc.), easy to imitate.

At the age of three Comrade Ogilvy had refused all toys except a drum, a sub-machine gun and a model helicopter. At six—a year early, by a special relaxation of the rules—he had joined the Spies; at nine he had been a troop leader. At eleven he had denounced his uncle to the Thought Police after overhearing a conversation which appeared to him to have criminal tendencies. At seventeen he had been a district organizer of the Junior Anti-Sex League. At nineteen he had designed a hand grenade which had been adopted by the Ministry of Peace and which, at its first trial, had killed thirty-one Eurasian prisoners in one burst. At twenty-three he had perished in action. Pursued by enemy jet planes while flying over the Indian Ocean with important despatches, he had weighted his body with his machine-gun and leapt out of the helicopter into deep water, despatches and all—an end, said Big Brother, which it was impossible to contemplate without feelings of envy. Big Brother added a few remarks on the purity and singlemindedness of Comrade Ogilvy's life. He was a total abstainer and a non-smoker, had no recreations except a daily hour in the gymnasium, and had taken a vow of celibacy, believing marriage and the care of a family to be incompatible with a twenty-four-hour-a-day devotion to duty. He had no subjects of conversation except the principles of Ingsoc, and no aim in life except the defeat of the Eurasian enemy and the hunting-down of spies, saboteurs, thought-criminals and traitors generally.

Winston debated with himself whether to award Comrade Ogilvy the Order of Conspicuous Merit: in the end he decided against it because of the unnecessary cross-referencing that it would entail.

Once again he glanced at his rival in the opposite cubicle. Something seemed to tell him with certainty that Tillotson was busy on the same job as himself. There was no way of knowing whose job would finally be adopted, but he felt a profound

onviction that it would be his own. Comrade Ogilvy, un-
magined an hour ago, was now a fact. It struck him as curious
hat you could create dead men but not living ones. Comrade
Ogilvy, who had never existed in the present, now existed in the
past, and when once the act of forgery was forgotten, he would
exist just as authentically, and upon the same evidence, as
Charlemagne or Julius Caesar.

1949.

NOTES

SHOOTING AN ELEPHANT. From: *New Writing* 1st series No. 2
(1936)
Shooting an Elephant.

p. 25 l. 7 *betel juice:* It is a very common habit in the East to chew betel leaf wrapped round parings of the areca nut (often called the betel nut); a little lime is sometimes added. The habit is said to help mastication, sweeten the breath and ease the pangs of hunger. It stimulates a copious flow of red saliva and blackens the teeth.

p. 26 l. 7 *British Raj:* rule, supremacy of Britain in Eastern countries.

p. 26 l. 8 *sæcula sæculorum:* to the end of time, for ever.

p. 26 l. 25 *in terrorem:* to cause terror, to frighten.

p. 26 l. 27 " *must* ": state of frenzy during mating season.

p. 26 l. 28 *mahout:* the man who drives and looks after an elephant.

p. 27 l. 26 *Dravidian:* belonging to certain races of Southern India.

p. 32 l. 28 *dahs:* A dah or dáo is a knife used mainly by the hill tribesmen of India and neighbouring countries. It has a blade about eighteen inches long, narrow at the haft, broad and square at the tip. It is usually carried unsheathed in the waistband.

DOWN THE MINE. From: *The Road to Wigan Pier* (1937)
England, Your England.

p. 34 l. 1 *pace:* with all deference to.

SKIRMISH IN SPAIN. From: *Homage to Catalonia* (1938).

p. 46 l. 1 *Benjamin:* Orwell's commanding officer, Captain Levinski, a Polish Jew.

p. 46 l. 10 *Mills bomb:* an oval-shaped hand-grenade which explodes only after the withdrawal of a metal pin.

p. 46 l. 20 *Torre Fabian:* a nearby farm-house.

p. 46 l. 24 *Kopp:* the Belgian Commandante, George Kopp.

p. 47 l. 3 *Shock Troopers:* several hundred refugee Germans serving with P.O.U.M. were organized into special battalions called Batallons de Choque.

p. 51 l. 24 *uralite:* the material of which the bomb casings were made.

p. 52 l. 8 *Dardanelles:* the ancient Hellespont separating Asia from Europe; scene of a disastrous campaign in 1915–16 when the Anglo-French armies tried unsuccessfully to defeat the Turks.

p. 53 l. 13 *Poum:* Partido Obrero de Unificacion Marxista.

MARRAKECH. From: *New Writing* (1939)
                    England, Your England.

p. 64 l. 30 *lucerne:* a leguminous plant resembling clover; purple medick.

THE ENGLISH CLASS SYSTEM. From: *The English People.*

p. 68 l. 2 *Dr. Goebbels:* German Minister of Propaganda under the Hitler régime.

p. 69 l. 3 *parvenus:* upstarts who have gained wealth or power rapidly.

POLITICS AND THE ENGLISH LANGUAGE.
                    From: *Horizon* No. 76 (April, 1946)
                    Shooting an Elephant.

p. 77 l. 7 *as gentle as any sucking dove: A Midsummer Night's Dream,* I. ii. 83.

p. 79 l. 20 *cul de sac:* a street, passage, etc., with only one open end; a situation from which there is no escape or outlet.

p. 79 l. 20 *ancien régime:* social system and government of monarchical France before the French Revolution.

p. 79 l. 20 *deus ex machina:* in ancient Greek tragedy, the sudden appearance of a God to solve the complications of the plot; a sudden intervention to solve a difficulty.

p. 79 l. 20 *mutatis mutandis:* with necessary alteration of details.

p. 79 l. 20 *status quo:* the existing state of things.

p. 79 l. 21 *gleichschaltung:* equality, parity.

p. 79 l. 21 *weltanschauung:* conception of the world, outlook on life.

p. 81 l. 9 *Marshal Pétain:* the puppet dictator of France under German domination during the 1939–45 war.

p. 84 l. 19 *White Papers:* official Government reports.

p. 89 l. 8 *Stuart Chase:* American economist and author. Orwell is probably thinking of Chase's book *The Tyranny of Words* (1938), reissued in a revised edition as *The Power of Words* in 1954.

WRITERS AND LEVIATHAN. From: *Politics and Letters* (1948)
England, Your England.

p. 90 l. 11 *Zhdanov:* Andrei Alexandrovich Zhdanov, 1896–1948. Head of Lenin Communist organization in 1934, he became secretary of the Central Committee of the Communist Party.

p. 91 l. 29 *Joyce:* James Joyce, 1882–1941. His best-known works are: *Dubliners* (1914); *Portrait of the Artist as a Young Man* (1917); *Ulysses* (1922); *Finnegan's Wake* (1939).

p. 91 l. 29 *Henry James:* 1843–1916. His novels include: *Roderick Hudson* (1875); *Portrait of a Lady* (1881); *The Spoils of Poynton* (1897); *The Wings of the Dove* (1890); *The Ambassadors* (1903). He wrote many short stories, the most famous of which is *The Turn of the Screw*

WHY I WRITE. From: *Gangrel* (1947)
England, Your England.

p. 99 l. 28 *Kitchener:* Secretary of State for War, 1914–16 and responsible for the rapid expansion of the British Army during those years.

p. 99 l. 29 *Georgian style:* the Georgians were a group of poets who published five anthologies between 1912 and 1922 and included such writers as Rupert Brooke, John Drinkwater, Walter de la Mare, W. W. Gibson, John Masefield and W. H. Davies.

p. 100 l. 6 *vers d'occasion:* verses written for a special occasion.

p. 100 l. 9 *Aristophanes:* Greek writer of comedies who lived c. 400 B.C.

p. 100 l. 20 *narcissistic:* excessive admiration of oneself.

POETRY AND THE MICROPHONE. From: *New Saxon Pamphlets* (1945)
England, Your England.

p. 110 l. 9 *Arnold Bennett:* the reference is to Bennett's *Literary Taste*, Chapter IX.

p. 112 l. 12 *Sweeney Agonistes:* an unfinished poem by T. S. Eliot (1932).

p. 113 l. 32 *A. P. Herbert:* Sir Alan Patrick Herbert, humorous writer and former Member of Parliament.

p. 114 l. 1 *A.B.C.A.:* Army Bureau of Current Affairs; responsible during the 1939–45 war for lectures, discussions, publications, etc. on current affairs for H.M. Forces.

p. 115 l. 7 *Professor Joad:* 1891–1953. Head of the Department of Philosophy at Birkbeck College, University of London. A popular broadcaster and writer of numerous books on philosophy and controversial questions of social and political life.

BOYS' WEEKLIES. From: *Horizon* No. 3 (March, 1940)
                              Inside the Whale
                              Critical Essays.

Anyone interested in the subject of this essay will find it discussed in E. S. Turner's *Boys Will be Boys* (Michael Joseph, 1948) and Geoffrey Trease's *Tales out of School* (Heinemann, 1948).

p. 118 l. 6 *B.O.P.:* *Boy's Own Paper* (described by Geoffrey Trease as "perhaps the only English juvenile periodical which has ever really succeeded in combining moral policy, good writing and genuine popularity.")

p. 118 l. 21 *Sexton Blake and Nelson Lee:* detectives in juvenile fiction.

p. 120 l. 13 *frabjous:* a nonsense word used by Lewis Carroll in his poem "Jabberwocky".

p. 122 l. 11 *Gunby Hadath:* John Edward Gunby Hadath, 1871–1954, a writer of many schoolboy stories.

p. 122 l. 11 *Desmond Coke:* 1879–1931. A master for many years at Clayesmore school and a writer of schoolboy stories, the best known being *The Bending of a Twig.*

p. 122 l. 15 *O.T.C.:* Officers' Training Corps.

p. 122 l. 18 *Stalky & Co.:* by Rudyard Kipling (1899).

p. 127 l. 21 *Mons and Le Cateau:* On 23rd August, 1914, a defensive battle was fought at Mons by the British to allow a French retreat. Three days later a battle was fought at Le Cateau to check the German pursuit after Mons.

p. 127 l. 24 *Lord Peter Wimsey:* the detective hero of many stories by Dorothy L. Sayers.

p. 128 l. 30 *babu:* native clerk who writes English.

p. 137 l. 24 *Sax Rohmer:* writer of thrillers, many with an eastern background; e.g. the Fu Manchu series

p. 141 l. 9 *Navy League:* an association formed to secure naval protection of British subjects and commerce and to teach the history and traditions of the sea. To-day, one of its duties is to help in the administration of the Sea Cadet Corps.

p. 141 l. 30 *Sapper:* pen-name of H. C. McNeile.

p. 141 l. 30 *Ian Hay:* pen-name of Major-General John Hay Beith.

p. 142 l. 5 *laissez-faire:* the principle of non-interference by a government with the actions of individuals, especially in trade and industry.

p. 142 l. 20 *Lord Camrose:* Chairman of the *Daily Telegraph* and Vice-Chairman of the Amalgamated Press.

CHARLES DICKENS. Extract from: "Charles Dickens", a long essay in
Inside the Whale
Critical Essays.

p. 146 l. 5 *longueurs:* over-long tedious passages.

p. 146 l. 28 *necrophilia:* unnatural love of death and the dead.

p. 147 l. 5. *Sweeney Todd:* a very popular Victorian melodrama. Tod Slaughter, whose touring company specialized in melodrama, is specially associated with this play. He took over the Elephant and Castle Theatre (opened in 1872) for three years, 1924–6.

p. 149 l. 29 *rococo:* excessively florid and ornate.

p. 153 l. 28 *Manon Lescaut: Histoire du Chevalier des Grieux et de Manon Lescaut,* by the Abbé Prévost (1731).

p. 153 l. 29 *Salammbô:* novel by Gustave Flaubert (1862).

p. 153 l. 29 *Carmen:* novel by Prosper Mérimée (1847), better known in its adapted form as an opera by Bizet (1875).

p. 154 l. 11 *Peter Bezoukhov:* one of the chief characters in Leo Tolstoy's *War and Peace* (1868).

p. 154 l. 14 *Bloom:* one of the two principal characters in James Joyce's *Ulysses* (1922).

p. 154 l. 14 *Pécuchet:* one of the principal characters in Flaubert's *Bouvard et Pécuchet* (1881).

p. 154 l. 34 *Frank Fairleigh:* novel by Francis Edward Smedley (1850).

p. 154 l. 34 *Mr. Verdant Green: The Adventures of Mr. Verdant Green, an Oxford Freshman,* a novel by Edward Bradley (1853).

p. 154 l. 34 *Mrs. Caudle's Curtain Lectures:* lectures on domestic problems and Mr. Caudle's shortcomings given by Mrs. Caudle to her husband when he is trying to go to sleep. Written by Douglas William Jerrold and published in *Punch* (1845).

p. 156 l. 24 *Smiles:* Samuel Smiles 1812–1904. Author of *Self-Help, Character, Thrift, Duty* and a number of biographies.

p. 157 l. 6 *Thackeray's Laura:* Laura Bell, the heroine of Thackeray's *The History of Pendennis.*

p. 157 l. 11 *antinomianism:* (Gk. *anti*-against; *nomos*-law). The Antinomians are Christians who believe that moral law is not binding, faith alone being sufficient for salvation.

THE SPORTING SPIRIT. From: *Tribune* (late 1945)
Shooting an Elephant.

THE RE-WRITING OF HISTORY. From: *1984.*

Orwell's imaginary world of 1984 is divided into three totalitarian super-states, Eurasia, Eastasia and Oceania, permanently at war with one another. Britain, now called Airstrip One, is controlled by the Party which governs through its four Ministries of Truth, Peace, Love and Plenty, concerned respectively with news and entertainment, war, law and order, and economic affairs. The main character of the book, Winston Smith, works in the Ministry of Truth re-writing news items in old newspapers to fit the current Party policy.

Winston and Julia, a colleague in the Ministry, fall in love and secretly conspire against the Party, only to be trapped and tortured until not even the ashes of either their love or their revolt remain.

p. 163 l. 2 *telescreen:* ". . . an oblong metal plaque like a dulled mirror which could be dimmed but there was no way of shutting it off completely. . . . The Telescreen received and transmitted simultaneously. Any sound . . . above the level of a low whisper would be picked up by it." Anyone within the field of vision of a telescreen could be seen as well as heard.

p. 163 l. 3 *speakwrite:* an instrument which converted speech into writing.

p. 163 l. 24 *Newspeak:* the official language of Oceania. See Appendix to *1984.*

p. 164 l. 15 *Big Brother:* the mythical leader of the Party, "black-haired, black-mustachio'd, full of power and mysterious calm."

p. 165 l. 30 *palimpsest:* parchment or other material on which two or more writings are found, one superimposed on the other.

p. 167 l. 17 *Two Minute Hate:* Each day two minutes are devoted to organized hatred of Emmanuel Goldstein, the Enemy of the People. He is supposed to be a renegade leader of the Party whose teachings are responsible for all treacheries, sabotage and heresies against the Party. His face is flashed on to all telescreens against a background of marching Eurasian soldiers and the viewers are roused to frenzy by contrived propaganda.

p. 169 l. 11 *Ingsoc:* Newspeak for "English Socialism".

p. 169 l. 28 *Floating Fortresses:* heavily-armed fortifications guarding strategic points on the sea lanes.

p. 172 l. 6 *Spies:* an organization of children who were encouraged to spy on adults (especially their parents) and on each other.

p. 172 l. 7 *Thought Police:* Secret Police who used every available means, including the Telescreens, to discover actions and thoughts which deviated from official Party policy.

p. 172 l. 9 *Junior Anti-Sex League:* an organization of young people which advocated complete celibacy for both sexes and suppression of all sexual feelings

A SELECT BIBLIOGRAPHY

A. BOOKS BY ORWELL

Down and Out in Paris and London (1933). Autobiography
Burmese Days * (1934). Novel.
A Clergyman's Daughter (1935). Novel.
Keep the Aspidistra Flying (1936). Novel.
The Road to Wigan Pier * (1937). Sociology, politics and auto-biography.
Homage to Catalonia (1938). History and autobiography.
Coming up for Air (1939). Novel.
Inside the Whale † (1940). Essays.
The Lion and the Unicorn: Socialism and the English Genius (1941). Political pamphlet.
Animal Farm: a fairy story (1945). Satire.
Critical Essays † (1946). Essays.
The English People (1947). Essays. ("Britain in Pictures" series.)
Nineteen Eighty-Four * (1949). Novel.
Shooting an Elephant † (1950). Essays.
Such, Such were the Joys † (1953). Autobiography and essays.
England, Your England † (1953). Essays.

NOTE

1. The books in the above list were published by Secker and Warburg apart from (*a*) *The English People,* which was published by Collins and is out of print, and (*b*) titles marked †, which are out of print.
2. The bulk of the material originally included in the books which are out of print is now available in *The Collected Essays, Journalism and Letters of George Orwell,* edited by Sonia Orwell and Ian Angus, Secker and Warburg, 1968.
3. The books marked * are also published in Heinemann Educational editions—*The Road to Wigan Pier* with an introduction by Richard Hoggart, *Nineteen Eighty-Four* (in the Modern Novel Series) with an introduction by Stephen Spender, and *Burmese Days* (also in the Modern Novel Series) with an introduction by Malcolm Muggeridge.

B. BOOKS ABOUT ORWELL

1. Tom Hopkinson. *George Orwell.* Longmans, Green & Co. (for the British Council and the National Book League). 1953. pp. 40. (Writers and their Work No. 39.)
2. Laurence Brander. *George Orwell.* Longmans, Green & Co. 1954. pp. 212.
3. John Atkins. *George Orwell.* John Calder. 1954. pp. 347.
4. Christopher Hollis. *A Study of George Orwell: the man and his works.* Hollis and Carter. 1956, pp. viii+212.

C. Articles, etc. about Orwell

Of the many articles that have been written about Orwell and his work, I have found the following most useful.

1. Wyndham Lewis. *The Writer and the Absolute*. Methuen. 1952. pp. 153–193.

2. George Woodcock. *The Writer and Politics*. Porcupine Press. 1948. pp. 111–124.

3. *Scots Chronicle* 1951 (formerly *Burns Chronicle*). Burns Federation, Kilmarnock. pp. 7–14. "George Orwell" by Richard Rees.

4. G. H. Phelps. *Living Writers*. Sylvan Press. 1947. pp. 106–115. "George Orwell" by V. S. Pritchett.

5. *The Cornhill Magazine* No. 996. Summer 1953. pp. 450–470. "George Orwell—Dark Side Out" by Tom Hopkinson.

6. *World Review*, June 1950. A special number devoted to Orwell containing excerpts from his unpublished notebooks, a personal memoir of Orwell by T. R. Fyvel, a note by Bertrand Russell, and revaluations of five of Orwell's books by Malcolm Muggeridge, John Beavan, Stephen Spender, Tom Hopkinson, Herbert Read and Aldous Huxley.

7. Lionel Trilling. *The Opposing Self*. Secker & Warburg. 1955. pp. 151–172. "George Orwell and the Politics of Truth."